THE OBSERVER'S
POCKET SERIES

THE OBSERVER'S BOOK
OF SHIPS

The Observer's Books

THE OBSERVER'S BOOK OF

SHIPS

By
FRANK E. DODMAN

Describing over
ONE HUNDRED TYPES
with 96 line drawings, 16 colour plates
and 16 plates of photographs

FREDERICK WARNE & CO. LTD.
FREDERICK WARNE & CO. INC.
LONDON · NEW YORK

Printed in Great Britain

PREFACE

THE ship generally has a long working life and the observer is therefore likely to see ships of a great variety of ages up to thirty years or more. Since the first edition of this book there have been a number of innovations and some of these have affected general appearance.

The engines of an increasing number of oceangoing cargo liners, and also passenger ships, are placed either right aft or so that most of the cargo space is forward of the engine room. The navigation bridge on some of the new "super" tankers is incorporated in the poop superstructure, and the resultant loss of visibility is offset to some extent by a much higher bridge. A still further development has been the introduction of a navigation tower to replace the usual bridge; a television camera fitted in the ship's stem assists visibility forward. New and strange funnel shapes continue to appear but the twin "stove-pipe" seems to be popular and can be seen on passenger liners, cargo vessels, tankers and tugs.

Experiments with automation have been mainly concerned with bridge control of the engines and so far have not affected the appearance of the ships. In the future, partially or completely automatic ships will be afloat; navigation in the open seas, engine maintenance, loading and discharging of cargoes, catering, anchor work and other operations may be carried out automatically.

With increasing use of road transport fewer general cargoes are available and there has been a further reduction of coastal services between British ports. Bulk cargoes of oil have not diminished as some power stations have changed from coal to oil fuel. In this and other spheres the demand for oil and petrol has meant more coastal and estuarine tankers.

A number of cross-Channel packets have been converted to carry many more cars and new car ferries are beginning to operate between this country and the Continent and Ireland, and from the Scottish mainland to the Hebrides. The stern trawler has been introduced into the fishing fleets of several nations with great success, and a new type of vessel—the fish factory trawler—is likely to affect the pattern of the fishing industry.

For economic and other reasons nuclear power for merchant ships has been slow to develop. The United States Government is building up a tremendous fleet of nuclear warships—aircraft carriers, cruisers, frigates and submarines. Britain has four "Polaris" submarines on order

5

to add to the existing group of nuclear "attack" submarines. Fresh conceptions of war at sea have resulted in some new types of warship, wholesale scrapping of earlier types, and changes in the function of many others. Guided missiles seem to be rapidly taking the place of conventional guns. Three British post-war cruisers are to lose half their armament of 6-in. guns in order to carry four helicopters on each.

The sailing ship is often regarded as a thing of the past, but ship enthusiasts have been delighted that in recent years square-rigged ships have been built as schoolships. At long last, Great Britain is to have a large sail-training vessel —not, it is true, a square-rigger, but a staysail schooner with three square sails on the foremast.

This new edition gives details of the changes mentioned and includes a good deal of other new material in the text and many new line drawings. The six plates showing the colours of shipping companies have been re-drawn and re-arranged and most of the other colour and black and white plates are new.

My thanks are due to the many shipping companies who have provided me with information on their funnel, house-flag and hull colours. I should like to express my gratitude to the following companies who have helped me by lending material for the plates: Ben Line, Black Funnel Line, B.P. Tanker Co. Ltd., British Railways (Southern Region), British Trawlers' Federation, James Burness & Sons, Ltd. (Thoresen Car Ferries), the Cunard Steam-Ship Co. Ltd., and the P. & O.-Orient Line.

Thanks are also due to the French and United States Naval Attachés in London, and the Ministry of Defence (Admiralty), for their assistance in lending photographs of warships, and to the Controller, H.M. Stationery Office, for his permission to reproduce the flags and a selection of signals from the International Code of Signals.

As on previous occasions I should like to thank those readers who have written, from all over the world, offering their criticisms and suggestions, which as far as possible have been incorporated in this new edition.

Poole, Dorset   FRANK E. DODMAN

CONTENTS

LIST OF PLATES

*All the line drawings, together with the unacknowledged colour and half-tone plates,
except nos. XXIV and XXV, are by the author*

8

1 — GENERAL INFORMATION

INTRODUCTION

THE observer's powers of observation, and his knowledge of ships, generally pass through the following stages:

(a) Recognition of the main *groups*: merchant ships, warships, fishing vessels, pleasure vessels, sailing vessels, harbour craft.

(b) Recognition of the main *types* within these groups, so that he knows the difference between a passenger liner and a cargo liner, a cruiser and a destroyer, a trawler and a drifter.

(c) Recognition of the *varieties* within each type—the difference between a fruit carrier and a fast cargo liner, a guided missile destroyer and an anti-submarine destroyer, a distant-water trawler and a near-water trawler, a barquentine and a topsail schooner.

With his expanding knowledge of types he acquires some skill in estimating the *tonnage*, *length* and *speed* of almost any ship he sees. At a later stage, by the hull form, funnel shape, character of superstructure and type of ventilator, davit or crane, he is able to guess at the approximate *date of building*.

Only at an advanced stage is he aware of some of the *national characteristics* in design (often difficult to describe) which may distinguish a French passenger-cargo liner from a Dutch vessel of the same type, or a Russian destroyer from a U.S.N. destroyer. He begins to know the *company character* of many merchant ships and immediately recognizes a Blue Funnel or a Clan liner by design alone. An experienced observer knows many *individual* ships and can state their owners, nationality, tonnage, speed, service and many other details of interest.

At the same time the observer gradually develops his knowledge of flags. He identifies *national flags* from the familiar "Red Duster" to the flags of South American and new-born African states. It would be impossible to know all the thousands of *house flags*, *funnel* and *hull colours* but the observer will learn a surprisingly large number, from the distinctive lavender hull, and red and black funnel, of the Union-Castle Line to some of the one-ship companies and Continental coasters.

In a pocket book of this size there is no room for merchant, naval and fishing fleet lists, but the drawings, photographs and notes provide information on many aspects of ships which will be of service to the observer who pursues his interest in the docks, along the shore, at sea—or even from the air.

9

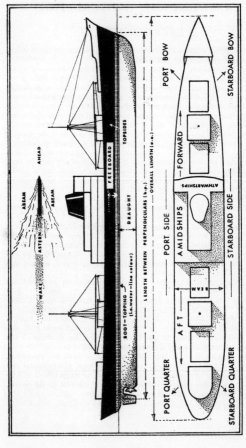

Fig. 1. Some nautical terms.

GLOSSARY OF NAUTICAL TERMS

MANY other terms are described, or illustrated, on Figs. 1 and 2, and on the drawings showing the parts of a merchant ship, sailing ship and yacht.

ATHWARTSHIPS. From one side of the ship to another—across the ship.

BALLAST. Sand, gravel or water carried by a ship when she is without cargo, to keep her propeller sufficiently submerged. Most vessels are fitted with water tanks and pumps specially for this purpose. Iron or lead weights placed in a yacht's bottom to counterbalance the heel when sailing.

BILGE. The curve of a hull where it changes from the side to the bottom. Some vessels have bilge keels to prevent rolling.

BULWARK. Steel or wooden wall round the ship's sides, giving protection to the deck.

CABLE. Approximately one-tenth of a nautical mile, or 200 yds.

CAMBER. The athwartships curve of a ship's deck. Exactly like the camber of a roadway.

COMPANION. Staircase or ladder down a hatchway. A ladder which can be lowered at ship's side to give access to water or quay level from deck.

DAVITS. Small cranes or apparatus for lifting and lowering ship's lifeboats. The oldest and simplest type is a pair of curved steel pillars. Later types have patent mechanical devices for speedier and more efficient lowering.

DOCKING BRIDGE. A platform at the stern for an officer to assist in controlling the ship's movements during docking operations. Usually connected by telegraph to the navigating bridge.

FLARE. The upward curve of the ship's side at the bows

GOALPOST MAST. Twin masts or sampson posts with a cross bar.

HATCHWAY. Opening in the deck through which cargo is loaded, or any opening giving access to space below decks. Steamers' hatchways are covered by hatch-boards, beams, and tarpaulins, or patent steel hatches. The yacht's or cabin cruiser's hatchway is covered by a sliding hatch.

KNOT. A nautical mile per hour.

NAUTICAL MILE. 6,080 ft. One minute of latitude at the Equator.

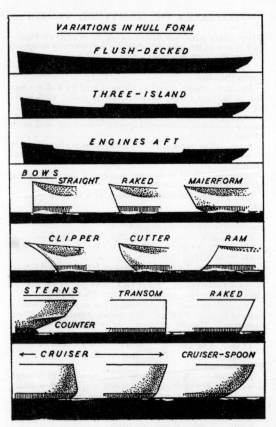

FIG. 2. Variations in hull form

PLIMSOLL OR LOAD LINE. Marks painted on the sides of a merchant ship to indicate the safe depth to which she may be loaded (see Fig. 3). The Ministry of Transport is responsible for the load-line regulations for British ships.

QUARTER. The ship's sides near the stern.

SHEER. The fore-and-aft curve of a ship's decks, rising towards the bows and stern. A warship's deck usually rises towards the bows only.

STRAKE. A horizontal line of plating or planking on the ship's sides. A rubbing strake is a permanent hard-wooded band along the ship's sides to protect the plating from chafing against quays and piers: a characteristic feature of the coaster and cross-Channel ship.

TRIM. The way the ship "sits" in the water, i.e. on an even keel, down by the head, or down by the stern.

TRUCK. Round piece of wood at the top of a mast.

WEATHER DECK. Uppermost deck of the hull—not superstructure.

WELL DECK. Deck space between either forecastle and bridge or bridge and poop.

Some abbreviations:

S.S.	Steamship	D/F	Direction Finder
M.V.	Motor Vessel	W/T	Wireless Telephony or Wireless Telegraphy
M.S.	Motor Ship		
S.Y.	Steam Yacht	A.B.	Able-bodied seaman
T.S.	Turbine Steamer or Training Ship	H.M.S.	Her Majesty's Ship
		I.N.	Indian Navy
R.M.S.	Royal Mail Ship	P.N.	Pakistan Navy
R.Y.S.	Royal Yacht Squadron	R.A.N.	Royal Australian Navy
M.N.	Merchant Navy	R.C.N.	Royal Canadian Navy
F.V.	Fishing Vessel	R.N.	Royal Navy
T.S.S.	Twin Screw Ship	R.N.L.I.	Royal National Lifeboat Institution
o.a.	Length overall		
b.p.	Length between perpendiculars	R.N.R.	Royal Naval Reserve
		R.N.V.R.	Royal Naval Volunteer Reserve
g.t.	Gross register tonnage		
dwt.	Deadweight	U.S.S.	United States Ship

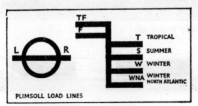

FIG. 3. Plimsoll load lines

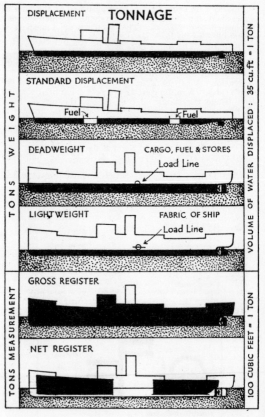

FIG. 4   Tonnage

14

TONNAGE

SHIP tonnage sometimes confuses the layman, particularly when he finds that one ship can have five different figures, the highest often three times larger than the lowest. A medium-sized freighter could have the tonnage figures 10,000, 7,500, 3,000, 5,200, and 3,500, and the diagrams opposite show, in a very much simplified way, how the different tonnages are calculated. Any comparison between tonnage figures must obviously refer to the same sort of tonnage for each of the ships concerned.

It is important to distinguish between the two kinds of "tons": one is weight avoirdupois and the other is equivalent to 100 cu. ft. of enclosed space. With regard to merchant ships, *gross*, *net* and *deadweight* tonnage figures are normally used. There is no hard-and-fast relationship between these figures, and unless ships are of the same type with the same functions comparisons are likely to be misleading. For example:

Type			Gross	Net	Dead-weight
Freighter	.	.	20,000	3,000	7,000
Tanker	.	.	6,700	4,000	10,000
Passenger Liner	.	.	20,000	12,000	10,000

DISPLACEMENT TONNAGE. This represents the total weight of the ship and everything on board. The volume of water displaced varies a little according to whether the water is salt, fresh, or in particular parts of the world. This tonnage is not used for merchant ships but always for warships. Since 1920 standard displacement has been the official figure, that is, the full displacement less the weight of fuel and reserve feed water. All warship tonnages given in this book are standard displacement.

DEADWEIGHT (dwt.). This is the weight in tons avoirdupois (or 20 cwt.) of the cargo, stores, fuel, etc., carried by a merchant ship when down to her loading marks (Plimsoll line, *see* page 13). It is equal to loaded displacement less the weight of the ship, the latter being the lightweight tonnage. The deadweight tonnage of a ship is a good indication of her cargo-carrying and earning capacity.

GROSS REGISTER (g.t.). The total cubic capacity of all enclosed space at 100 cu. ft. to the ton. Used for general purposes and in national maritime registers.

NET REGISTER. Measured in the same way as gross tonnage, the net register is the capacity of enclosed space *less* that of the engine and boiler rooms, crew accommoda-

15

tion, stores, and all spaces necessary for the working of the ship. In other words, it is the cubic capacity of all earning space, and it is on this tonnage figure that most harbour dues and other charges are calculated.

METHODS OF MECHANICAL PROPULSION

Steam Reciprocating Engines. The first passenger steamship was the *Comet* of 1812. She was propelled by a simple 4-h.p. engine driving at first two pairs of paddles, and later one. Fuel consumption was large and consequently her trips were short. All early steamships suffered from the handicap of excessive fuel consumption. The simple engine developed into the two-cylinder compound engine and eventually became the triple-expansion compound engine as we know it today. The steam, generated in Scotch fire-tube boilers, passes successively through a small high-pressure cylinder, a medium-pressure and a large low-pressure cylinder. The triple-expansion engine is slow but economical and reliable. It is now being replaced by the diesel motor in most classes of vessel.

Steam Reaction Turbines. Acting on a principle similar to that of the water wheel, the steam—generated in water-tube boilers—passes through numerous fine nozzles on to small blades fixed round the rim of a cylinder, thus forcing it to revolve. The average turbine revolves at a speed of about 4,000 r.p.m. and before this power can be transmitted to the propeller shaft the rotational speed must be reduced through single or double reduction gearing to a speed of about 100 r.p.m. This mechanically simple type of engine is efficient, quiet and smooth-running, and it is particularly suitable for fast passenger liners although it is used for some fast cargo liners, tankers, cross-Channel packets and most warships.

Electric Propulsion. In electrically driven ships the shafts are connected up to electric motors for which the power is generated by either diesel- or steam-turbine-driven generators. Turbo-electric machinery is often employed for large ocean-going tankers, for a small number of passenger liners and a number of tugs. The latest British trawlers are driven in this way.

Diesel Motors. The general principle of the marine motor engine is similar to that of the motor-car internal-combustion engine except that the oil fuel is ignited by

16

compression. Compared with the steam engine, the fuel consumption is much lower. An added advantage is that fuel is not consumed when the ship is lying in port. Each year diesels are fitted to an increasing number of ships from 100-ton coasters up to 25,000-ton liners.

GAS TURBINES. In 1947 a British gunboat was fitted with gas turbines for seagoing tests and early in 1952 the British tanker *Auris* (12,000 tons dwt.) was driven across the Atlantic by an experimental gas turbine fitted in addition to diesel-electric machinery and later re-engined with a single 5,500-h.p. gas turbine. The American freighter *John Sergeant* was the first pure gas-turbine merchant vessel. Some British fast Patrol Boats are powered by gas turbines, and a new type of propulsion machinery, combining gas turbines with steam turbines, is now in use in fast escort vessels, frigates and some freighters.

NUCLEAR REACTORS. This latest form of marine propulsion is based on the use of nuclear fuel, which, in minute bulk, can give a tremendous cruising range. The first atomic ship was the U.S. submarine *Nautilus* which completed a voyage of 50,000 miles without re-fuelling. The American *Savannah*, the first nuclear powered cargo vessel, is described on page 51. The first British nuclear powered ship is the submarine *Dreadnought*. Many difficulties have to be faced before this form of power can be an economical proposition for the merchant ship, but plans for giant nuclear powered tankers and other forms of merchant ship are in preparation.

An important innovation of recent years has been the bridge control of ship's engines so that one man can manoeuvre the vessel alongside a quay. Another new development has been the closed circuit television with the camera fitted into the ship's stern so that the master, in the wheelhouse, can more easily control docking operations.

Fig. 5. BUOYAGE SYSTEM OF THE UNITED KINGDOM

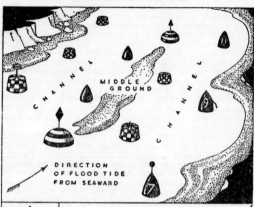

CHANNEL

MIDDLE GROUND

CHANNEL

DIRECTION OF FLOOD TIDE FROM SEAWARD

Starboard-hand buoys are conical in shape and painted in a single colour. They mark the *right*-hand side of a channel entering from seaward and the *left*-hand when proceeding seawards.

Port-hand buoys are *can* or *barrel*-shaped and are either parti-coloured or a single colour different from the starboard buoys. They mark the *left*-hand side of a channel entering from seaward and the *right*-hand when proceeding seawards.

Middle ground buoys are spherical and painted in horizontal white and coloured stripes. They mark sandbanks or shoals in the middle of a channel or the division between two channels.

Wreck buoys are painted green with WRECK in large white letters. They may be conical, can or spherical shaped according to which side a vessel may safely pass.

Fig. 6. NAVIGATION LIGHTS FOR VESSELS OVER 150 FT. IN LENGTH

Anchor or riding lights. An all-round white light on the forestay 20 ft. to 40 ft. above the hull and at the stern a similar white light 15 ft. lower than the forward light.

ON THE PORT BEAM: WHITE · RED · WHITE

ON THE STARBOARD BEAM: WHITE · GREEN · WHITE

GREEN   GREEN   RED   RED

FROM STARBOARD BOW: RIGHT AHEAD   FROM PORT BOW

Steaming lights. A white light on the foremast 20 ft. to 40 ft. above the hull visible ahead and two points $(22\frac{1}{2}°)$ abaft either beam; a similar white light on the mainmast at least 15 ft. higher than the forward light. *Side or bow lights,* placed lower than the white lights and visible right ahead and two points abaft the beam, *red* on the *port* side and *green* on the *starboard* side. A white *stern light* is shown by a vessel when being overtaken.

2 — FLAGS

INTERNATIONAL CODE (Plate I)

THE present version of the International Code of Signals came into being in 1934 and is used by all nations at all times. The Royal Navy has its own code, although many of the same flags are used.

SIGNAL LETTERS

Besides the letter values shown in Plate I, each flag has a signal value. For example, the letter **D** also means "Keep clear of me—I am manœuvring with difficulty." Every ship, and even many small yachts, has a four-letter identification signal. British ships have either **G** or **M** as the first letter. The letter **F** represents France, **PA** or **PI** Holland, and **K**, **N** or **W** the United States of America.

Every phrase likely to be used at sea is represented by a group of code letters. Each ship carries the official International Code books which contain all these recognized signals. If it is necessary to send an unusual signal, perhaps containing someone's name, the words may be spelt out letter by letter. To economize in flags, substitute flags are used; for instance, in the signal indicating the port of Plymouth, **A M P M**, the last letter would be indicated by a substitute flag instead of repeating the letter **M**.

Signals flags should always be flown from a point where they can be read without obstruction from masts or stays. If more than one point is used the signal reads from forward aft.

On festive occasions in port, ships of all types may "dress ship," that is, fly all the code flags on a taut line hoisted from the stem or bowsprit over the trucks of the masts down to the stern.

In the Royal Navy code flags are arranged in a prescribed order; other ships have no ruling for dressing ship, but for the sake of uniformity they can use a standard arrangement devised by the Admiralty.

SIGNAL FLAGS: SELECTION OF SIGNALS

SINGLE-LETTER SIGNALS

A I am undergoing a speed trial. **B** I am taking in or discharging explosives. **C** Yes (Affirmative). **D** Keep clear of me—I am manœuvring with difficulty. **E** I am altering my course to starboard. **F** I am disabled. Communicate with me. **G** I require a pilot. **H** I have a pilot on board. **I** I am altering my course to port. **J** I am going to send a message by semaphore. **K** You should stop your vessel instantly. **L** You should stop. I have something important to communicate. **M** I have a doctor on board. **N** No (Negative). **O** Man overboard. **P** (Blue Peter). *In harbour:* All persons are to repair on board as the vessel is about to proceed to sea (flown at foremast). *At sea* (by flashing): Your lights are out or burning badly. **Q** My vessel is healthy, I request a free pratique. (A vessel arriving in British waters from abroad must declare whether she is "healthy" or "suspect." Pratique is permission to hold intercourse with the port. If there is a case of infectious disease on board, the signal QQ is hoisted, signifying "My ship is suspect.") **R** The way is off my ship; you may feel your way past me. (The vessel is stationary, i.e. not under way.) **S** My engines are going full speed astern. **T** Do not pass ahead of me. **U** You are standing into danger. **V** I require assistance. **W** I require medical assistance. **X** Stop carrying out your intentions and watch for my signals. **Y** I am carrying mails. **Z** To be used to address or call all shore stations.

A SELECTION OF TWO-LETTER SIGNALS

AM Accident has occurred, I require a doctor. **NC** I am in distress and require immediate assistance. **SC** What is the name of your vessel?

SELECTION OF THREE-LETTER SIGNALS

E C E What course are you steering? **P Y U** Good voyage.

FOUR-LETTER SIGNALS

Ports. **A A A S** Aberdeen.   **A J J O** Liverpool.
A G J V Glasgow.
Ships. **G B T T** *Queen Mary.*   **P G G F** *Nieuw Amsterdam.* **G Y K S** *Caronia.*

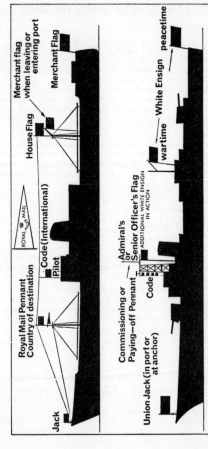

Fig. 7. Positions of flags worn by merchant ships and warships

BRITISH FLAGS AND ENSIGNS
(Plate IV)

FLOWN by warships and merchant ships, unless otherwise stated, these flags are worn on the ensign staff at the stern (Fig. 7). Small vessels sometimes wear them at the gaff of the mainmast.

British ensigns are twice as long as they are wide. Some foreign ensigns are similar in proportion, but some are much shorter in relation to their width.

In port merchant flags and ensigns are hoisted at 8 a.m. between March and September or at 9 a.m. between September and March, and they are hauled down at sunset. At sea ensigns may be worn as long as there is sufficient light for them to be seen. They must be worn when a ship is entering or leaving port at any time of the day or night. British ships of over fifty tons are compelled by law to carry and wear the national merchant flag.

1. WHITE ENSIGN. Ensign of the Royal Navy, worn by H.M. ships, shore establishments and boats of the Royal Yacht Squadron.

2. RED ENSIGN. National merchant flag of the British Merchant Navy. Worn by any British-owned ship, yacht or small boat. Known as the "Red Duster." Also used as the ensign of dominions, each distinguished by their emblems, e.g. the stars of Australia. Trinity House, Humber Conservancy and other institutions also wear this flag with an emblem on the fly.

3. BLUE ENSIGN. Worn as the merchant flag by merchant ships which have among their crews a certain number of officers and men belonging to the Royal Naval Reserve. Members of certain yacht clubs may by special warrant wear this ensign with the club emblem on the fly. Lloyd's, Custom House, Mersey Docks and Harbour Board, etc., also wear this flag with their badges on the fly. Royal Army Service Corps vessels wear a blue ensign with crossed swords on the fly.

4. ROYAL AIR FORCE. Worn by R.A.F. stations, Air Sea Rescue launches, and other vessels belonging to the R.A.F.

5. ROYAL FLEET AUXILIARY ENSIGN. Worn by fleet auxiliaries and oilers.

6. TRINITY HOUSE. The badge on the fly of the Red Ensign. Used by lighthouse tenders and pilot boats.

7. IRISH LIGHTS. Ensign used in the same way as No. 6 above.

8. COMMISSIONERS OF NORTHERN LIGHTS. Lighthouse service of Scotland and the Isle of Man. Worn only when Commissioners are on board lighthouse tenders. Normal ensign is blue with white lighthouse. This flag, like the Red Duster, is twice as long as it is deep.

9. UNION JACK. Worn at the jackstaff of British warships while at anchor. The pilot flag is a Union Jack with a white border, worn at the jackstaff by merchant ships or at the foremast when a pilot is required.

MERCHANT FLAGS (Plate V)

1. Argentina
2. Belgium
3. Finland
4. Eire
5. France
6. Germany (E. and W.)
7. Honduras
8. Italy
9. Japan
10. Liberia
11. Netherlands
12. Panama
13. United States of America
14. Poland
15. Portugal
16. U.S.S.R.
17. Spain
18. Sweden
19. Denmark
20. Norway
21. Greece
22. Israel

FLAGS OF CONVENIENCE (Plate V)

Since the last war a large number of merchant ships have been registered under the flags of Honduras (7), Liberia (10), Panama (12) and Costa Rica. These small countries, previously with little or no mercantile marine, have shipping laws with much lower standards than those of Great Britain and America. Taxation is considerably less and thus the shipowners are able to operate with better profits when their vessels are registered under flags of convenience. Many big British companies are now operating associated companies under these flags and that of Bermuda. Some of the world's largest tankers are owned by companies flying the Liberian and Panamanian national flags.

COLOURS OF SHIPPING
COMPANIES

THE coloured plates show a selection of funnel colours with their designs or symbols, hull colours and companies' house flags.   The use of red, yellow, green and blue takes no account of a company's individual version of a colour; for example, yellow is capable of a wide range of variation but is here represented by a bright yellow throughout.   An increasing use of white, grey or pale green instead of black means the hull colours shown may not be accurate.

Information in the text gives (a) reference number of the relevant plate; (b) name of the company (English version first); (c) port of registry; (d) classification of ships' names; (e) main service routes.

PASSENGER LINERS (Plate VIII)

(Companies whose fleets include one or more passenger liners over 20,000 g.t.)

1. ROYAL ROTTERDAM LLOYD (Koninklijke Rotterdamsche Lloyd N.V.).   Rotterdam.   Mainly Netherlands East Indies place names.   Round-the-world passenger and worldwide cargo services.   Tankers.

2. HAMBURG-ATLANTIC   LINE.   Hamburg.   T.S. *Hanseatic*.   Hamburg, Channel ports and New York.

3. THE UNION-CASTLE MAIL STEAMSHIP CO. LTD. London. — *Castle*.   Mail, passenger and cargo, England and Continent to South and East Africa. Subsidiary of the British and Commonwealth Shipping Co. Ltd.

4. THE CUNARD STEAM-SHIP CO. LTD.   Liverpool. —*ia* except for the two *Queens*.   Passenger, mail and cargo from Liverpool, Southampton, London, Greenock, Havre to New York and Canada.   Cargo also to U.S. Gulf ports, Great Lakes and the Mediterranean. Some green hulls have white line above boot-topping.

5. FRENCH LINE (Compagnie Générale Transatlantique).   Havre.   Misc. names.   Express passenger from France and U.K. to U.S.A., West Indies and South America.   France to Morocco and Tunisia.

Fig. 8. *Burgee of the British and Commonwealth Shipping Group.* The Union-Castle Line (Plate VIII, 3), Clan Line (Plate XII, 11), Bullard King & Co., Ltd., and other subsidiary companies are amalgamated under the title of British and Commonwealth Shipping Company. Ships of the various companies wear this burgee above their own individual house flags.

Freight to U.S.A., Central and South America, Great Lakes and Baltic ports and Russia.

6. UNITED STATES LINES COMPANY. New York. *American* — except for *United States* and *America*. New York to Southampton and Havre with passengers and mail. Worldwide freight services, some with *Pioneer* vessels.

7. ORIENT STEAM NAVIGATION CO. LTD. London. *Or*—. U.K. to Australia and Far East. Cruises. Amalgamated with P. & O.S.N. Co. White hulls.

8. PENINSULAR & ORIENTAL STEAM NAVIGATION CO. London. Mainly Eastern names. London to India and Australia, China and Japan. Cruising. Tankers (Trident Tankers Ltd., *O*—*a*, black funnel with black trident in a white diamond).

9. ROYAL MAIL LINES LTD. London. Misc. names. U.K. to South America, Central America, South America and N. Pacific ports.

10. NEW ZEALAND SHIPPING CO. LTD. London or Plymouth. Maori names. U.K., Continent, Canada and U.S.A. to and from Australia and New Zealand.

11. SWEDISH AMERICAN LINE (Svenska Amerika Linien). Gothenburg. —*holm*. Passenger service Baltic to U.S.A. and Canada, cargo Scandinavia to ditto and Gulf of Mexico.

12. CANADIAN PACIFIC STEAMSHIPS LTD. London. *Empress of* — and *Beaver* — for cargo vessels. Liverpool and Greenock to Canada. Cruises.

13. HOLLAND-AMERICA LINE (Nederlandsche-Americkaansche S.M.N.V.). Rotterdam. —*dyk*, —*dam*. Rotterdam to New York, N. Pacific coast, Mexico.

14. SHAW SAVILL & ALBION CO. LTD. Southampton. —*ic*. U.K. to New Zealand and Australia. Round-the-world cruises.

15. ROYAL DUTCH LINE ("Nederland" N.V.S.M.). Amsterdam. Misc. names. Round-the-world passenger services. Continent to Far East.

16. GREEK LINE (General Steam Nav. Co. Ltd. of Greece). Andros. Various names. Bremerhaven, Southampton to New York and latter to Mediterranean. Cruises.

17. NORDDEUTSCHER LLOYD. Bremen. —*stein* except for large passenger liners, *Bremen* and *Berlin*. Germany to U.S.A., Central and South America. Australia and Far East.

18. "ITALIA" SOCIETA PER AZIONI DI NAVIGAZIONE. Genoa. Italian personal and place names. Mediterranean to N., S. and Central America and Pacific.

TANKERS
(Plate IX)

Companies primarily concerned with the transportation of oil in bulk. Passenger and dry cargo companies also owning tankers are indicated elsewhere.

1. ANDERS JAHRE. Sandefjord, Norway. *Ja*—. Whaling, tanker, dry cargo and passenger ships.

2. OVERSEAS TANKSHIP (U.K.) LTD. (Caltex Trading & Transport Co. Ltd.). London. Also under Panama, Dutch and French flags. *Caltex* followed by names of large towns or cities.

3. NIARCHOS GROUP under flags of Greece, Liberia and Panama. Also World Tanker Co. Ltd. *World*—. Bulk carriers.

4. HUNTING & SON LTD. (also Hunting (Eden)

Tankers Ltd.). Newcastle-on-Tyne. —*field.* **Also** general cargo carrier services.

5. ESSO PETROLEUM CO. LTD. London. Under flags of many other countries. *Esso* — (towns or countries).

6. NAESS GROUP. British, Dutch and Liberian flags. *Naess* —.

7. A. P. MOLLER. Copenhagen. — *Maersk,* also cargo liners.

8. REGENT PETROLEUM TANKSHIP CO. LTD. (subsidiary of Texaco, U.S.A.). London. *Regent* —.

9. SOCONY MOBILE OIL CO. INC. Under flags of several countries. *Mobil* —, — *Arrow.*

10. ATHEL LINE LTD. (subsidiary of United Molasses). Liverpool. *Athel*—, also bulk sugar carriers.

11. B.P. TANKER CO. LTD. London. *British* —. Also Tanker Charter Co., Clyde Charter Co. Ltd.

12. COUNTIES SHIP MANAGEMENT CO. LTD., London, and LONDON AND OVERSEAS FREIGHTERS LTD. *London* —.

13. ONASSIS GROUP. Liberian flag. Various company titles.

14. SHELL TANKERS LTD. Large tanker fleets under flags of several countries. Names of shells, *San* —, *Shell* —.

15. SHELL-MEX AND B.P. LTD. London. *Shell* —, *B.P.* — (second word an occupation). Distributors for Shell and B.P. groups.

16. ROWBOTHAM & SONS (MANAGEMENT) LTD. London. —*sman.* Coasting and home trade tankers.

17. METCALF MOTOR COASTERS LTD. London. Coasting and home trade tankers, also dry cargo vessels. Personal names followed by *M.*

18. ADMIRALTY. Fleet replenishment oilers and fleet attendant oil tankers. *Tide*—, —*leaf, Wave* —, *Eddy*—, —*ol,* — *Ranger.*

BRITISH OCEANGOING FREIGHTERS AND PASSENGER/CARGO LINERS

(Plate XII)

1. P. Henderson & Co. Glasgow. Burmese place names. Glasgow, Liverpool, Swansea to Egypt and Rangoon via Suez.

2. Anchor Line Ltd. Glasgow. —*ia*. Glasgow to U.S.A., U.K. to Egypt, Pakistan and India.

3. Hain Steamship Co. Ltd. London. *Tre*—. General trading.

4. Booth Steamship Co. Ltd. Liverpool. Male saints. Liverpool to S. America, New York to West Indies, London to Brazil and Peru. Cruises.

5. Donaldson Line Ltd. Glasgow. —*ia*. U.K. to E. Canada and River Plate.

6. Moss Hutchison Line Ltd. Liverpool. Egyptian place names. Liverpool, Glasgow, Bristol Channel to Bordeaux, Peninsula and Mediterranean. Tankers.

7. Walter Runciman & Co. Ltd. (Moor Line Ltd.). London. —*moor*. Tramps.

8. Thos. & Jas. Harrison Ltd. Liverpool. Professions and trades. London, Liverpool, Glasgow to Red Sea, S. and E. Africa, Central and South America.

9. Houlder Brothers & Co. Ltd. London. — *Grange*, etc. U.K. to S. America (River Plate), London to S. Africa. Tankers and ore carriers.

10. British India S.N. Co. Ltd. London. —*a*. U.K. to India and Far East, Africa, Australasia. Tankers and educational cruise ships.

11. Clan Line Steamers Ltd. Glasgow. *Clan* —, *King* —. U.K. to Africa and Far East. Australia to Africa. India to S. America. Subsidiary of The British and Commonwealth S.C. whose burgee is flown over the Clan house flag. (*See* Fig. 8.)

12. Furness Withy & Co. Ltd. London. —*more*, *Pacific* —. Liverpool to Canada and U.S.A., New York to Bermuda, Manchester and Glasgow to N. Pacific ports. Cruises.

13. Prince Line Ltd. (Furness Group). London.

— *Prince*. U.K. to Mediterranean, U.S.A. to Far East via Panama.

14. THOS. AND JNO. BROCKLEBANK LTD. Liverpool. Indian names, *M*—. U.K. to India, Ceylon, India to U.S. Gulf ports, U.K. to Gulf.

15. FRANK C. STRICK & CO. LTD. London. —*istan*. U.K. and Continent to Persian Gulf.

16. GLEN LINE LTD. (Glen & Shire Line). Liverpool. *Glen*—, —*shire*. U.K. and Continent to Far East.

17. BIBBY LINE LTD. Liverpool. —*shire*. U.K. to Egypt, Sudan, Ceylon and Burma. Trooping.

18. PORT LINE LTD. London. *Port* —. U.K., U.S.A., Canada to and from Australia and New Zealand. Subsidiary of Cunard Line.

(Plate XIII)

19. SIR WILLIAM REARDON SMITH & SONS LTD. (and LEEDS S. CO. LTD.). Bideford. — *City*. Worldwide tramping.

20. FEDERAL STEAM NAVIGATION CO. LTD. London. English counties. U.K., U.S.A. and Canada to Australasia. Tankers.

21. BLUE STAR LINE LTD. London. — *Star*. U.K. to S. America, S. Africa, Australia, New Zealand and W. Indies. Tankers.

22. MANCHESTER LINERS LTD. (Furness Group). Manchester. *Manchester* —. Manchester to Canada, U.S.A. and Great Lakes.

23. ELDER DEMPSTER LINES LTD. Liverpool. West African place names. U.K. and Continent to Mediterranean, U.S.A., Canada to W. and S.W. Africa, India to W. Africa.

24. THE PACIFIC STEAM NAVIGATION COMPANY. Liverpool. South American names. U.K. to W. Indies and W. coast of S. America via Panama. Subsidiary of Royal Mail Lines Ltd. Tankers.

25. MACANDREWS & CO. LTD. London. Spanish names, mainly *V*—. U.K. to Spain and Morocco, Sicily and W. Italy.

26. LYLE SHIPPING CO. LTD. Glasgow. *Cape* —. General tramps. Some grey hulls.

27. BEN LINE STEAMERS LTD. Leith. *Ben*—. U.K. and Continent to Far East.

28. BANK LINE LTD. (Andrew Weir & Co. Ltd.). Glasgow. —*bank*. U.K. to South Sea Islands, India to W. Africa, China, Japan to Africa, U.S. Gulf to Australia and New Zealand, U.S.A. to Japan and Malaya, etc.

29. ELDERS & FYFFES LTD. Glasgow. Central and S. American rivers. U.K. to W. Indies and Cameroons.

30. H. HOGARTH & SONS LTD. Ardrossan. *Baron* —. Glasgow to Lisbon. General trading.

31. ELLERMAN LINES LTD. London, Liverpool or Glasgow. *City of* —, —*ian*. Worldwide services under several companies in Ellerman group, all with same funnel and hull colours but distinguished by different house flags.

32. JAMES NOURSE LTD. London. Indian river names. General trading and tramps, tankers.

33. ROPNER SHIPPING CO. LTD. West Hartlepool, —*by*, and POOL S. CO. LTD., —*pool*. Tramps and tankers.

34. PALM LINE LTD. London or Liverpool. — *Palm*. U.K. to W. Africa.

35. BLUE FUNNEL LINE (Alfred Holt & Co.). Liverpool. Greek mythological names. U.K. and Continent to Far East, Australia, W. Australia to East Indies, China and Japan, U.S.A. to Philippines, China and Japan, New York and Halifax to Malaya and Indonesia via Suez Canal.

36. LAMPORT & HOLT LINE LTD. Liverpool. Artists, writers, musicians. Glasgow, Liverpool, etc., to S. America, New York to Manchester, W. Indies, Brazil.

BRITISH SHORT SEA PASSENGER, CARGO AND EXCURSION SERVICES

(Plate XVI)

1. COAST LINES LTD. Liverpool. — *Coast*. Extensive *cargo* services between ports in British Isles. *Passenger* service in summer months between Liverpool, London and Eire via Southampton. Coast Lines Organization includes eleven other coastal companies in U.K.

2. CURRIE LINE LTD. Leith. —*land*. *Cargo* services between Leith, Grangemouth, London, Liverpool and Manchester and Scandinavia, N. Germany and the Mediterranean. *Passenger*, Leith and Grangemouth to Copenhagen, Hamburg and Bremen, London to Lisbon.

3. GENERAL STEAM NAVIGATION CO. LTD. London. Names of birds for *cargo* vessels; service English ports to France, Low Countries, Germany, Denmark and Mediterranean. *Excursions* from London to Southend, Margate and Calais in summer only.

4. DAVID MACBRAYNE LTD. Glasgow. Mainly *Loch* —. *Cargo* from Glasgow to Inner and Outer Hebrides. Numerous *passenger* and *car ferry* services in the Clyde area and Hebrides.

5. RED FUNNEL STEAMERS LTD. (Southampton, Isle of Wight and South of England Royal Mail Steam Packet Co. Ltd). *Passenger*, *car ferry* and *cargo* services between Southampton and Cowes. Summer excursions in Southampton Water and along South Coast.

6. BELFAST STEAMSHIP CO. LTD. Belfast. *Ulster* —. Belfast and Liverpool *passenger* service. *Cargo* (including livestock) N.W. ports of England and Belfast.

7. ELLERMAN'S WILSON LINE LTD. (Ellerman Group). Hull. —*o*. *Passenger* services from Hull, London, Liverpool and Manchester to Scandinavian ports. *Cargo* U.K. to Scandinavia, Russia and Mediterranean.

8. ISLE OF MAN STEAM PACKET CO. LTD. Douglas.

Manx names. *Passenger* and *car ferry* service between Douglas and Liverpool, Ardrossan, Heysham, Dublin and Belfast. *Cargo* Liverpool and Isle of Man.

9. BURNS & LAIRD LTD. Glasgow or Liverpool. (Coast Lines Group). *Passenger*, Glasgow to Belfast, Dublin. *Scottish* —. *Cargo*, Clyde to N. Ireland and Eire. *Lairds*—.

10. NORTH OF SCOTLAND, ORKNEY & SHETLAND SHIPPING CO. LTD. (Coast Lines Group). Aberdeen. *St.* —. Leith to Aberdeen, Kirkwall, Lerwick and N. Isles of Shetland.

11. NEW MEDWAY STEAM PACKET CO. LTD. Rochester. Summer *excursion* services only in Thames estuary; operated last paddler in area until 1963.

12. BRITISH RAILWAYS BOARD. London. Miscellaneous names. Numerous cross-Channel *passenger*, *train ferry*, *car ferry* and *cargo* services between Great Britain, the Continent and Eire.

13. THE CALEDONIAN STEAM PACKET CO. LTD. Glasgow. (Scottish Region of the Br.R.B.). *Maid of* —, Scottish names. Numerous *passenger*, *car ferry*, *cargo* and *excursion* services in the Firth of Clyde, Kyle of Lochalsh ferry to Skye.

14. COSENS & CO. LTD. Weymouth (associated with the S., I. of W. and S. of E. R.M.S.P. Co. Ltd.). Summer *excursions* Isle of Wight, Bournemouth and Weymouth.

15. UNITED BALTIC CORPORATION LTD. London. *Baltic* —. *Passenger* services, London and Hull to Gdynia and Baltic ports. *Cargo* as passenger but joint services with other lines to Mediterranean.

16. ASSOCIATED HUMBER LINES LTD. Hull. — *Abbey*. N.E. towns. *Passenger* and *cargo* Hull to Low Countries, Goole to same ports, Copenhagen, Hamburg, Bremen and Dunkirk.

17. P. & A. CAMPBELL LTD. Bristol. — *Queen*, *Glen* —. Summer *excursions* only in Severn estuary.

18. BRITISH & IRISH STEAM PACKET CO. LTD. Dublin. Irish place names. *Passenger*, *car ferry*, *cargo* and *livestock* between main Irish and English ports.

COASTAL AND SHORT SEA CARGO SHIPS

(Plate XVII)

1. CLYDE SHIPPING CO. LTD. (Coast Lines). Glasgow. Names of lighthouses. Glasgow, London, Belfast, Waterford, Bristol. Tugs at Glasgow and Greenock.

2. WILLIAM ROBERTSON SHIPOWNERS LTD. (Gem Line). Glasgow. Minerals and semi-precious stones. Coastwise services.

3. GEORGE GIBSON & CO. LTD. Leith. Scottish borders place names. Leith, Grangemouth, Dundee, Aberdeen, Middlesbrough to Belgium, Holland, France and Portugal.

4. F. T. EVERARD & SONS LTD. London. —*ity*. Dry cargo and oil coasters between British and Continental ports. Ships of GLEN & CO. now carry Everard house flag on black top of red funnel. —*a*.

5. STEPHENSON CLARKE LTD. London. English place names, mainly S. Managers of Central Electricity Generating Board and North Thames Gas Board. Coal and oil to power stations and gas works. Tankers.

6. WILLIAM SLOAN & CO. LTD. Glasgow. Scottish rivers. Glasgow to Belfast, Bristol, Cardiff and Swansea.

7. WM. FRANCE, FENWICK & CO. LTD. London. —*wood*. Coasting, short-sea, intermediate and deep-sea tramps.

8. LONDON & ROCHESTER TRADING CO. LTD. Rochester. —*ence*. Motor coasters, coastal barges, river motor barges, tugs and lighters.

9. WM. CORY & SON LTD. London. *Cor*—. Colliers, deep-sea tankers and ore carriers. Tugs.

10. COMBEN LONGSTAFF & CO. LTD. (Williamstown S. Co. Ltd.). London. —*brook*. Colliers.

11. NORTH THAMES GAS BOARD. London. *Fire*— and misc. names. Upriver colliers to serve gas works. Flatirons.

12. SOUTH EASTERN GAS BOARD. London. Towns in Home Counties. Colliers, N.E. coast and London.

13. JOHN KELLY LTD. Belfast. *Bally*—. Colliers.

35

14. CENTRAL ELECTRICITY GENERATING BOARD. London. *Pompey* —, *Fulham* —. Personal names associated with the industry. Colliers, coastal tankers.

15. THE DUNDEE, PERTH & LONDON SHIPPING CO. LTD. Dundee. Mainly Scottish place names. Dundee to London and Southampton, Great Lakes to Newfoundland.

16. CONSTANTINE SHIPPING CO. LTD. Middlesbrough. —*wood*. Colliers, short-sea and Mediterranean, general trading.

17. BRITISH & CONTINENTAL STEAMSHIP CO. LTD. Liverpool. Some bird names. Liverpool, Manchester, Barrow, Glasgow, Belfast to Low Countries ports and Dunkirk.

18. HUDSON STEAMSHIP CO. LTD. London. *Hudson* —. Colliers, N.E. coast to London, deep-sea general traders.

FISHING VESSEL PORT OF REGISTRY LETTERS

Selection of British and Irish Ports

A	Aberdeen	M	Milford Haven
AB	Aberystwyth		
AD	Ardrossan	NN	Newhaven (Scotland)
AH	Arbroath		
		OB	Oban
BCK	Buckie		
BF	Banff	PD	Peterhead
BM	Brixham	PE	Poole
		PW	Padstow
C	Cork	PWG	Port Glasgow
CF	Cardiff	PZ	Penzance
CK	Colchester		
CS	Cowes (Isle of Wight)	R	Ramsgate
CT	Castletown (Isle of Man)	RO	Rothesay
CY	Castlebay (Isle of Barra)	S	Skibbereen (Eire)
		SA	Swansea
		SC	Scilly Isles
D	Dublin	SE	Salcombe
DE	Dundee	SH	Scarborough
DK	Dundalk (Eire)	SR	Stranraer
DO	Douglas (Isle of Man)	SS	St. Ives
		SY	Stornoway (Isle of Lewis)
FD	Fleetwood		
FE	Folkestone	T	Tralee (Eire)
FY	Fowey	TH	Teignmouth
		TN	Troon
G	Galway		
GE	Goole	UL	Ullapool
GN	Granton		
GU	Guernsey	W	Waterford (Eire)
GY	Grimsby	WA	Whitehaven
		WD	Wexford (Eire)
H	Hull	WH	Weymouth
HH	Harwich	WK	Wick
HL	Hartlepool	WN	Wigtown
		WY	Whitby
IE	Irvine		
INS	Inverness	Y	Youghal (Eire)
		YH	Yarmouth
J	Jersey		
LH	Leith		
LK	Lerwick (Shetland)		
LN	King's Lynn		
LT	Lowestoft		
LY	Londonderry		

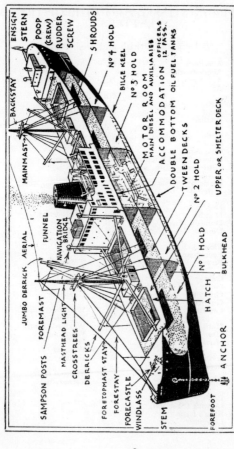

FIG. 9. Parts of a cargo vessel

SAMPSON POSTS
JUMBO DERRICK
FOREMAST
MASTHEAD LIGHT
CROSSTREES
DERRICKS
FORETOPMAST STAY
FORESTAY
FORECASTLE
WINDLASS
STEM
FOREFOOT
ANCHOR
HATCH
N° 1 HOLD
BULKHEAD
AERIAL
NAVIGATION
BRIDGE
FUNNEL
MAINMAST
BACKSTAY
ENSIGN
STERN
POOP (CREW)
RUDDER
SCREW
SHROUDS
N° 4 HOLD
BILGE KEEL
N° 3 HOLD
MOTOR ROOM
MAIN DIESEL AND AUXILIARIES
ACCOMMODATION
OFFICERS
12 PASS.
DOUBLE BOTTOM OIL FUEL TANKS
N° 2 HOLD
TWEEN DECKS
UPPER OR SHELTER DECK

3 — MERCHANT SHIPS

PARTS OF A CARGO VESSEL

THE hull of a typical cargo-carrier is a flat-bottomed steel structure divided into a number of watertight compartments by vertical steel walls called transverse bulkheads. These bulkheads separate the holds from the machinery space. The double bottom consists of an inner and outer skin with tanks between for oil fuel and water ballast. The machinery space of the motor ship takes up much less room than that of the average steamship with her engine room, boilers and coal fuel bunkers. The holds are divided horizontally by one or two decks with hatchways giving access to the lower holds. The passenger liner may have several decks and as many as fifteen transverse bulkheads. The *Queens* (*see* page 45) also have an inner and outer skin, several feet apart, on each side of the midship section of the hull.

The drawing—Fig. 9—shows a flush-decked vessel with a raised forecastle and raised poop and a compact bridge superstructure which comprises the navigating bridge, boat deck, and passengers' and officers' accommodation. The crew (rarely berthed in the forecastle) are accommodated in the poop. The derricks are capable of lifting three- to five-ton loads and many vessels are fitted with a jumbo derrick for weights of twenty tons or more. Each derrick is equipped with a steam or electric winch. The hatchways are covered by movable steel hatch-beams and wooden hatch-boards finally sealed with tarpaulins securely wedged along the hatch-coamings; many modern ships are equipped with labour-saving steel-hinged hatches. The conventional mast, with rigging of stays and shrouds, is now giving way to the self-supporting bipod mast (Plate VII, upper) which offers no obstruction and requires little maintenance.

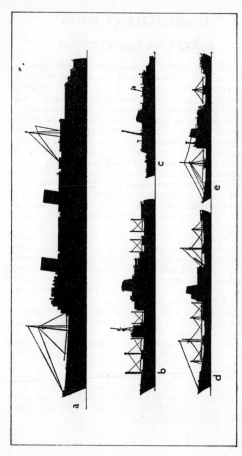

FIG. 10. Comparative silhouettes of merchant ships (I)

COMPARATIVE SILHOUETTES

(Fig. 10)

	Type	Date	Gross tonnage	Length overall in feet	Propulsion	Speed in knots	Service	Page ref.
a	TRANSATLANTIC PASSENGER AND MAIL LINER	1940 (Br.)	83,673	1,031	ST (4)	28¼	Southampton–Havre–New York	45
b	PASSENGER AND CARGO LINER	1959 (Br.)	20,348	584	M (2)	17½	U.K.–South America	51
c	TRAIN/CAR FERRY, BOW LOADING	1959 (Da.)	3,668	364	M	16	Great Belt, Denmark	63
d	FAST CARGO LINER	1959 (Br.)	11,463	550	ST	19	U.K.–Far East	53
e	FRUITER (BANANA CARRIER)	1959 (Br.)	6,159	445	ST	17	West Indies and U.K.	67

Nationality
Br.   British
Sp.   Spanish
Da.   Danish
Du.   Dutch
Sw.   Swedish
No.   Norwegian

Propulsion
ST   Steam turbines
M   Motor diesel engines
GT   Free-piston gas turbines
(2)   Twin screws
(4)   Quadruple screws

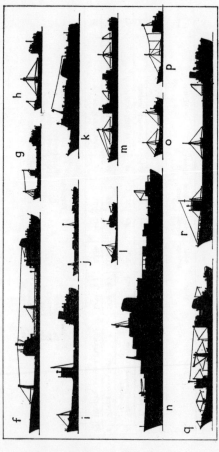

Fig. 11. Comparative silhouettes of merchant ships (II)

COMPARATIVE SILHOUETTES
(Fig. 11)

	Type	Date	Gross tonnage	Length overall in feet	Propulsion	Speed in knots	Service	Page
f	TANKER/BULK OIL CARRIER	1960 (Sp.)	21,247	652	ST	16	Middle East to British oil refineries	65
g	COLLIER	1959 (Br.)	1,092	220	M	11½	Coastwise, U.K.–Continent and N. Ireland	59
h	COASTER/SHORT SEA TRADER (GENERAL CARGO AND CONTAINER CARRIER)	1959 (Br.)	963	231	M	12	U.K. and Continent	53
i	ORE CARRIER	1960 (Br.)	6,990	427	GT	11	To Port Talbot, South Wales	57
j	COLLIER (UPRIVER COLLIER OR FLATIRON	1947 (Br.)	1,773	261	M	11	Coal to London power stations	79
k	CROSS-CHANNEL PACKET	1960 (Du.)	6,300	393	M (2)	23½	Harwich–Hook of Holland (day)	61
l	DISTANT WATER TRAWLER	1959 (Br.)	698	177	M	14½	Hull–N. Atlantic–Arctic	155
m	GENERAL TRADER OR TRAMP	1953 (Br.)	5,580	449	M	13	General cargo and tramping	53
n	PASSENGER AND MAIL LINER	1960 (Br.)	38,000	783	ST (2)	22½	Southampton–S. Africa	47
o	DUTCH COASTER	1959 (Sw.)	499	171	M	11½	North Sea and Baltic	59
p	COASTAL TANKER	1959 (Br.)	856	208	M	10	Southampton Water Refineries to depots	66
q	HEAVY LIFT CARGO SHIP	1960 (Br.)	8,846	488	M	16	General cargo—10, 15 and 110 ton derricks	Plate III
r	WHALE OIL FACTORY	1948 (No.)	18,631	616	M (2)	12½	Antarctic	69

43

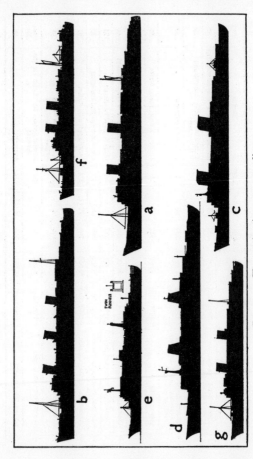

TWIN
FUNNELS

FIG. 12. Transatlantic passenger liners

44

TRANSATLANTIC PASSENGER LINER

(Plates II and XXVIII)

THE main features of these liners—the world's largest passenger ships—are the immensely long, high superstructure, the unimportant masts, few deck cranes or derricks, large number of lifeboats and the great length of enclosed promenade deck.

These ships keep strictly to the fixed routes between their terminal ports—such as Southampton, Cherbourg, Havre, Hamburg and New York—simply because their size entails special deep-water quays and special passenger, baggage, customs and other facilities. The "turn-around" may be only a few days, and to ensure the competent and smooth running of these floating luxury hotels, the replenishment of stores, cleaning of accommodation and many other tasks have to be done at high speed and with great efficiency. On occasion one of these large ships may be engaged in cruising.

		Flag	Gross tonnage	Length overall	Speed in knots	Approx. no. of passengers
a	Queen Elizabeth	Br. 1940	83,673	1,031	28½	2,300
b	Queen Mary*	Br. 1936	81,237	1,019	28½	2,040
c	United States	U.S. 1952	53,329	990	29 35 max.	2,000
d	France	Fr. 1961	66,000	1,035	31	2,000
e	Rotterdam	Ne. 1959	38,645	748	22	1,456
f	Mauretania	Br. 1939	35,677	773	23	1,170
g	Nieuw Amsterdam	Ne. 1938	36,667	759	21½	1,230
	Caronia (Plate II)	Br. 1948	34,183	715	22	932
Other vessels over 30,000 g.t. (not illustrated)						
	Leonardo da Vinci	It. 1960	33,340	761	23	1,326
	America	U.S. 1939	33,961	723	22	1,228
	Bremen (ex-Pasteur) (re-constructed 1959)	Ge. 1938	32,335	697	23	1,125
	Hanseatic (ex-Empress of Scotland, re-constructed 1958)	Ge. 1930	30,329	673	20	1,250
Building Q4 (Cunard) to replace Queen Mary		1967	58,550	960	29½	2,000

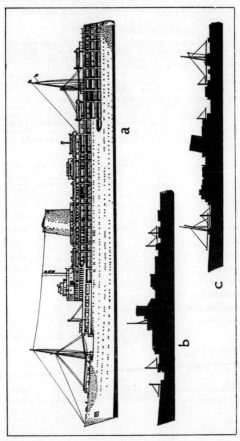

FIG. 13. Passenger liners (I)

PASSENGER LINER

(Plates XX, XXI and XXIV)

As the name suggests, this type of vessel is employed primarily for the carrying of passengers in any part of the world, but she is generally designed to carry a small amount of cargo. Size and silhouettes vary considerably and, with recent experiments in funnel design, some companies have adopted a type of funnel which helps identification.

The large drawing shows a passenger liner built for trade between Great Britain, Australia and New Zealand via the Suez Canal. Her open promenade decks suggest that she is employed in tropical waters; the ships on the North Atlantic routes have more protection against wind and weather.

The outline of the passenger liner may be broken by deck houses, boats and derricks. The two silhouettes opposite show passenger vessels with quite different shapes although they are approximately the same size. The *Orcades* (b) illustrates the modern tendency to place the tripod mast and funnel rather close together. The *Edinburgh Castle* (c) and *Pretoria Castle* carry only half as many passengers as the *Orcades* but much more cargo—a fact suggested by their larger number of derricks.

Illustrations (FIG. 13)

(a) *Iberia.* Built in 1954 for the P. & O. Line. 29,614 g.t. 718 ft. o.a. Geared turbines, twin screw, speed of 24·9 knots. Accommodation for 1,407 passengers. 4,000 dwt. cargo. Great Britain to Australia and Far East.

(b) *Orcades.* Built in 1948 for the Orient Line. 28,164 g.t. 709 ft. o.a. Geared turbines, twin screw, speed of 21·8 knots. Converted in 1964 to a "one-class" vessel for 1,635 passengers.

(c) *Edinburgh Castle.* Built in 1948 for the Union-Castle Line. 28,705 g.t. 747 ft. o.a. Geared turbines, twin screw, speed of 22 knots. Accommodation for 705 passengers on the Southampton to South Africa mail service.

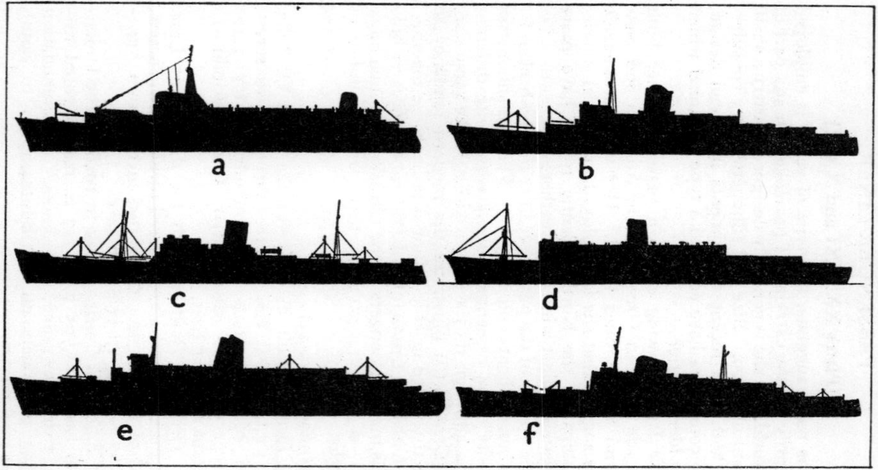

FIG. 14. Passenger liners (II)

Canberra and *Oriana*, owned by P. & O.-Orient Lines, are the largest liners on the run to the Far East. With speeds of 27½ knots they have reduced the passage time from Southampton to Australia by one week to three weeks only. They have similar specifications but differ a good deal in appearance. *Canberra* is propelled by turbo-electric machinery placed aft and has slender side-by-side funnels, but *Oriana*, propelled by double-reduction geared turbines, has her machinery amidships—her after funnel acts as an engine room ventilator. Both these twin-screw ships have a new arrangement of lifeboats which are fitted on a deck level lower than usual. They have aluminium superstructures, bulbous bows and transverse propulsion equipment at bow and stern to assist docking, and each liner carries well over two thousand passengers.

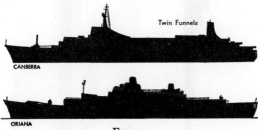

Twin Funnels

CANBERRA

ORIANA

FIG. 15

Canberra   45,000 g.t.   820 ft. o.a.   2,250 passengers.
Entered service 1961.   (Plate XXI)
Oriana   41,923 g.t.   804 ft. o.a.   2,184 passengers.
Entered service 1960

Illustrations (Fig. 14)

	Date	g.t.	ft. o.a.	kn.	Passengers
(a) *Southern Cross* Shaw Savill Line	1955	20,203	603	20	1,160
(b) *Carmania* and sisters Cunard	1954	21,637	608	20	940
(c) *Rangitane* New Zealand Line	1949	21,867	609	17	403
(d) *Queen of Bermuda* Furness Line (re-constructed 1962)	1933	22,501	580	20	731
(e) *Empress of Britain* Canadian Pacific (sold to Greek Line 1964)	1956	25,516	640	21	1,050
(f) *Flandre* C.G.T.	1951	20,469	599	23	709

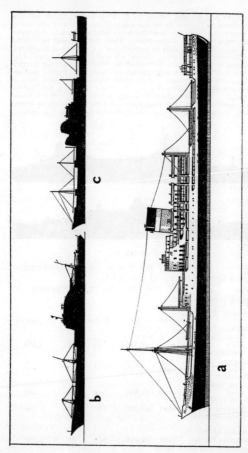

FIG. 16. Cargo-passenger liner

CARGO-PASSENGER LINER
(Plate XXIX)

ALTHOUGH most passenger liners carry some cargo, their main purpose is to cater for several hundred passengers at a speed of anything up to 30 knots. The smaller intermediate or cargo-passenger liner found on most of the world's trade routes is distinguished from the passenger liner by the much shorter superstructure and the greater number of derricks or deck cranes. As a rule the speed of such a ship is between 15 and 18 knots and the machinery is either steam turbine or diesel. The new experimental funnel designs have increased the variety of silhouettes, but the tendency is towards a compact superstructure and a squat funnel sometimes incorporated in the navigation bridge.

The *City of Port Elizabeth* (a), owned by the Ellerman Lines, was built in 1952 on the Tyne: she measures 13,363 g.t. with an overall length of 541 ft., Doxford-type diesels and twin screws giving her a speed of just over 16 knots. She has a curved and raked stem and a cruiser stern. She carries 100 passengers between London and South Africa.

The American *Savannah* (b) is the first nuclear-powered cargo-carrying ship. She is designed to carry 60 passengers and nearly 10,000 tons of cargo at a speed just over 20 knots, steaming for 300,000 miles without re-fuelling.

The French cargo-passenger liner *Caledonien* (c) is a vessel with a very low superstructure and a modern type of raked and domed funnel. Her diesels give her a speed of 16 knots carrying 241 passengers and cargo between Marseilles and Australia via the Panama canal.

CARGO LINER
(Fig. 17)

THE cargo liner runs to a fixed time-table between two or more ports. Any size between three and ten thousand tons gross, her silhouette is capable of many variations, although the solid-looking compact superstructure is common and the split superstructure is becoming something of a rarity on a modern vessel. The cargo liner's speed may be as high as 19 or 20

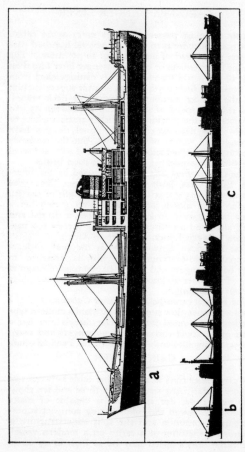

FIG. 17. Cargo liner

knots (see fast cargo liner, Fig. 10d and plate III).

The 17-knot ship (a) was built to operate between the Mersey and South and East Africa with a gross tonnage of 7,878 and a length of 502 ft. overall. She carries 10,000 tons of cargo and 12 passengers in excellent accommodation. Illustration (b) shows a modern trend—that of designing the cargo liner with engines aft—in a cargo liner built in 1959, 4,460 g.t., a length of 378 ft. overall, and a speed of $14\frac{1}{4}$ knots for service between Manchester and the Great Lakes through the St. Lawrence Seaway.

A new type of cargo liner, now building, is a fast 12,000-ton cargo and mail liner for the U.K.–South Africa route. Twin-screw, with a speed of $22\frac{1}{2}$ knots, she will be equipped to carry wine in bulk as well as general cargo.

TRAMP

THE term *tramp* indicates a category of employment rather than a specific type of vessel. The tramp ship is a general cargo, or bulk carrier, vessel employed to take cargo from port to port at any time and in any area according to the demands of the trade. Some tramp ships are modern well-equipped vessels such as that in Fig. 17c, which is a Spanish dual-purpose ship of 4,250 g.t. built in 1959 for tramping service all over the world. She is fitted with a laboratory, classroom and accommodation for training 24 engineer cadets.

SHORT SEA TRADER
(Figs. 11h and 20)

GENERALLY well under 3,000 tons, the short sea trader operates in the North Sea, Baltic, Channel or Mediterranean (or similar areas in other parts of the world). She may, like the cargo liner, run to a fixed schedule between ports. Machinery is either aft or amidships: the difference in appearance between the modern cargo liner and the short sea trader is becoming difficult to define as more and more of the former are built with engines aft. The short sea trader may carry coal or grain in bulk or general cargo and is usually fitted with efficient cargo handling gear in order to deal with all types of cargo—including containers—in ports with limited facilities.

53

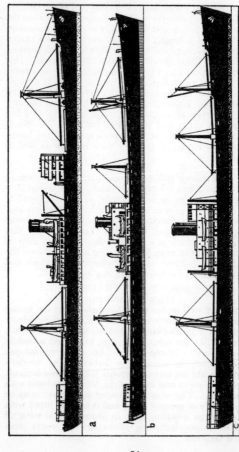

Fig. 18. Standard types of general cargo merchant ships

STANDARD TYPES OF MERCHANT SHIPS

DURING the two world wars thousands of new cargo ships were required to replace those lost by enemy action. Building had to be swift and was much simplified. In the Second World War the designs were better and more pleasing than the ugly American *Hog Island* sheerless type of the First World War. Valuable time was saved by the introduction of prefabrication, the extensive use of welding and standardization of parts.

The American-built *Liberty* type (Fig. 18b) is probably the best known of the second war standard types. Of the original 2,708 *Liberties*, a large number are still afloat, particularly in the tramp trade where they can earn better profits than the newer ships. The 7,000-ton *Liberty* is flush decked with a short, high superstructure and three masts. The Canadian-built *Fort* and *Park* types (a) and the American-built *Oceans* are similar in size to the *Liberty* but they have split superstructures. The third drawing (c) is of an American-built *Victory* type, 7,500 tons, which is about three knots faster than the above and distinguished by a larger composite superstructure and a long forecastle.

The British standard cargo liner was a 15-knot vessel of almost 10,000 tons gross with a short forecastle, composite superstructure, three masts forward and one aft and kingposts set against the after end of the bridge. For reasons of economy a British shipbuilding firm has recently produced plans for six standardized motor ships—three dry cargo, two bulk-carriers and one tanker.

The United States built a large number of C1 to C4 standard types for its own use. The first three have short, high superstructures and three holds forward and two aft with many variations of masts, kingposts and details of bridge. The C4 has engines aft.

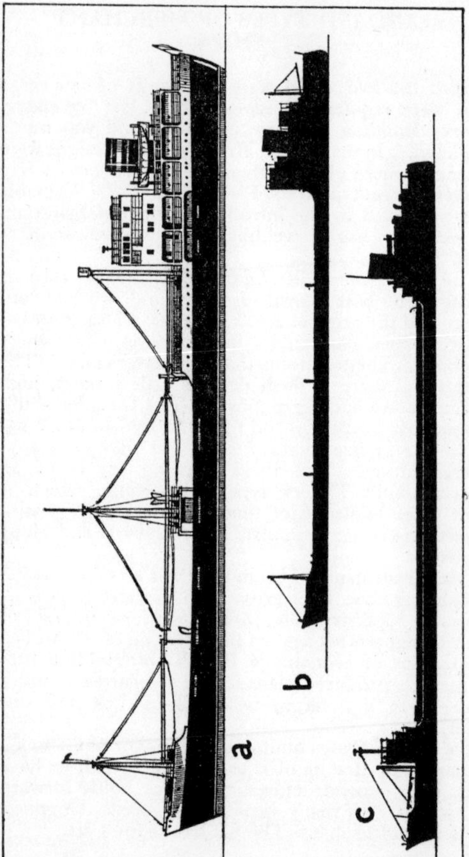

FIG. 19. Bulk carriers

BULK CARRIERS

(Plates XXXI and XXXII)

THE bulk carrier is a specially designed freighter employed for the exclusive carriage of oil, ore, molasses, latex, cement, sugar, bauxite, phosphates or coal. The oil tanker is described on page 65. The collier is usually a raised quarter deck coaster (Fig. 20) without derricks, as loading and discharging of coal is done by dockside cranes.

The bulk sugar carrier is a type developed in recent years. The *Sugar Importer* (Fig. 19a) is a modern motor ship of 3,960 g.t. carrying about 5,000 tons of sugar from the West Indies to London. She has an overall length of 353 ft. and is driven by two 8-cylinder British Polar diesels. The sugar is discharged by grabs and the hatch covers are of the combined rolling and pivoting type.

The bulk ore carrier is usually a large vessel with engines aft. The drawing (b) shows a British motor ship of 7,000 g.t. and a length of 427 ft. For the reason suggested above in connection with the collier, she has no derricks. The three projections are part of the gear which operates the hinged hatches.

The illustration (c) is the silhouette of a large single-screw turbine ore-carrier, the *Carl Schmedeman* (9,918 g.t.), which carries aluminium ore (bauxite) from Ocho Rios Bay, Jamaica, to Mobile in Alabama. She has stern self-unloading equipment capable of discharging her ore cargo at the rate of 1,400 tons per hour. Like the Great Lakes carriers her bridge is placed on the forecastle (Fig. 34).

Several oil tankers such as the *Sinclair Petrolore* (35,131 g.t.) have been designed to carry return cargoes of ore. Sailing under the Liberian flag (*see* Plate V) she has over a million cubic feet of ore space in her bottom and sides with self-unloading gear and two and a half million cubic feet of space for oil. She takes oil from the Persian Gulf to America, sails in ballast to Venezuela to load ore for Japan, and returns to the Gulf for more oil.

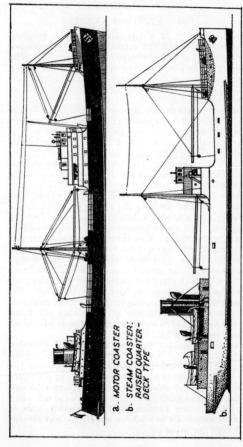

a. MOTOR COASTER

b. STEAM COASTER: RAISED QUARTER-DECK TYPE

FIG. 20. The coaster or short sea trader

THE COASTER AND SHORT SEA
TRADER
(Plates VI and VII)

THE coaster can be seen anywhere around our coasts, in any port, large or small, or tied up at a lonely up-river quay. Generally she is an all-purpose cargo carrier, although some coasters run to a regular time-table between certain ports and might be classed as specialized "liners." Many coasters are employed as colliers either on regular coastal or irregular short-sea routes. At the other extreme is the tiny *puffer* of the west coast of Scotland, where she is the only means of transporting cargo between many of the islands. Colliers designed for regular service between, for instance, a coal port in North-East England and a gas works or power station have no cargo handling gear (Plate VI, upper) but rely solely on dock grabs and other equipment.

The coaster may be up to 200 ft. in length with a gross tonnage of something under 2,000, and has powerful derricks and deck machinery capable of handling a variety of cargoes in small ports where there is little or no quayside machinery. Usually the machinery is aft so that the shaft tunnel is short and does not take up valuable space. Some vessels have a raised quarter deck—that is, the deck from the bridge to the poop is several feet higher than the forward well deck (*see* Fig. 20). This gives a better trim when the ship is fully loaded. All coasters have a rubbing strake on each side of the hull to protect it from damage by bumping while tied up to a quay wall.

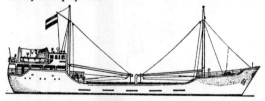

FIG. 21. Dutch coaster

During recent years the Dutch motor coaster has become a common type in European waters. Developed in Holland for operating in very shallow estuaries, rivers and canals, she has a shallow draught, engines and accommodation aft, a large hold, electric cargo machinery, and a strong hull to enable her to lie well on the ground at low water.

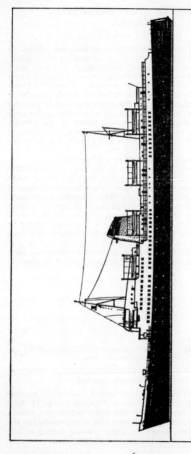

FIG. 22. Cross-Channel passenger and drive-on, drive-off car packet, *Maid of Kent* (4,413 g.t.), operating on the day service between Dover and Boulogne. Driven by turbines and twin-screws, she maintains a speed of 20 knots carrying 1,000 passengers and 180 cars. She has twin rudders aft, a bow rudder, a bow lateral-thrust unit and stabilizers. *See also* Fig. 11 (k).

CROSS-CHANNEL PACKET
(Plate XXV)

THE cross-Channel steamer or motor ship is similar in appearance and in function to the much larger passenger liners. She carries a large number of passengers and mail and a small amount of cargo on routes which demand accurate timing to fit in with train services. The ships built for day crossings carry about 1,500 passengers and have eight or ten lifeboats. The night ships, usually on a longer route, have accommodation for about 500 passengers. The *Maid of Kent*, built for the British Railways Board (Fig. 22), is a good example of a cross-Channel packet.

The cross-Channel packets have high-powered engines to maintain a speed of about 20 knots in all weathers. The prevailing weather conditions of the route have an important effect on the design of the ship. The introduction of Denny-Brown stabilizers on the latest cross-Channel ships has reduced rolling. An increasing number of "roll-on, roll-off" car ferries are being added to the cross-Channel fleets (Plate X, lower).

The following are some cross-Channel routes:

DAY	Dover – Calais; Ostend – Dover; Liverpool–Isle of Man; Stranraer–Larne
NIGHT	Harwich–Hook; Liverpool–Belfast; Glasgow–Belfast
DAY OR NIGHT	Weymouth–Channel Islands; Seattle–Vancouver – Victoria; Buenos Aires–Montevideo
DAY AND NIGHT PASSAGE	Harwich–Esbjerg; Newcastle–Bergen

Most of the crossings from the British Isles to Ireland and the Continent take less than 24 hours.

Two new types of fast passenger vessel have been introduced to cross-Channel and inter-island services. They are the hovercraft, which rides on a cushion of air, and the hydrofoil, which 'flies' over the surface of the water on wings fitted under the hull.

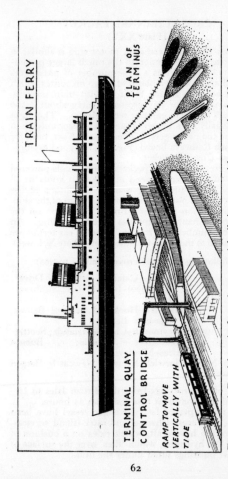

TRAIN FERRY

PLAN OF TERMINUS

TERMINAL QUAY
CONTROL BRIDGE

RAMP TO MOVE
VERTICALLY WITH
TIDE

FIG. 23. A Danish train ferry (2,950 g.t.) built in 1951 with a speed of 16½ knots for the service between Nyborg and Korsor. The lower drawing shows one form of pivoted ramp necessary in tidal waters

TRAIN FERRY
(Plate X)

THE train ferry is used only on a few short sea routes. With her broad beam, high superstructure and lack of sheer and derricks she is unmistakable. The essential feature is the long, clear deck equipped with two or more rail tracks, and with access at one end or both ends of the vessel. The boiler flues or engine exhausts are sometimes taken up to twin funnels placed near the ship's sides, to make the rail deck as large as possible.

To enable the deck rails to line up correctly with those on shore the hull is shaped to fit exactly into a terminal dock with a pivoted ramp which rises and falls with the tide.

The train ferry has passenger accommodation and dining saloons. On some overnight services the passengers remain in the train sleeping cars.

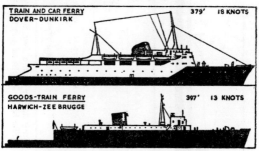

TRAIN AND CAR FERRY DOVER–DUNKIRK — 379' — 18 KNOTS

GOODS-TRAIN FERRY HARWICH–ZEEBRUGGE — 397' — 13 KNOTS

FIG. 24. Miscellaneous ferries

Train ferries carry London–Paris trains from England to the Continent via Dover and Dunkirk. In Denmark, with its numerous islands, the train ferry is an important part of the railway system. In the North American lakes there are many train ferries, and in order to maintain a full twelve-months' service these are fitted as icebreakers. Large train ferries carry 100 loaded wagons between New Orleans and Cuba, New Orleans and New Jersey, and Texas City and New York.

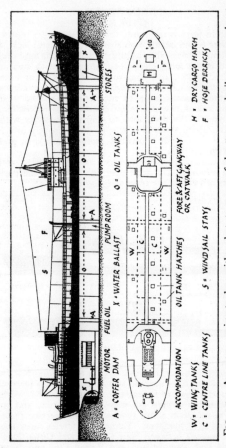

FIG. 25. An ocean-going tanker with a dwt. tonnage of about 30,000 built to carry about 28,500 tons of oil. She has a length of 523 ft. and a service speed of about 15 knots.

A = COFFER DAM MOTOR FUEL OIL PUMP ROOM O = OIL TANKS STORES

X = WATER BALLAST

ACCOMMODATION FORE & AFT GANGWAY H = DRY CARGO HATCH
      OR CATWALK F = HOSE DERRICKS

OIL TANK HATCHES S = WINDSAIL STAY

W = WING TANKS

C = CENTRE LINE TANKS

TANKER
(*See* Plate XI)

THE specialized carrier of oil in bulk is now one of the most important vessels in the world's merchant fleets. She is distinguished from the general cargo carrier by her long, low hull, island bridge and the after position of her engines. The three islands—forecastle, bridge and poop—are connected by light fore-and-aft bridges called *catwalks*. These are necessary as the low deck is frequently awash. As the tank tops are all watertight there is no danger of flooding when this happens.

Two longitudinal bulkheads and many transverse bulkheads divide the hull into numerous tanks. Each tank has a watertight hatch and a ventilator, and is connected by pipe-line to the pumping-rooms. In two or more positions are double bulkheads, providing narrow air space, called coffer dams. These coffer dams give strength and lessen the danger of fire spreading from the forecastle or engine room to the tanks. The dangerous swilling effect of a liquid cargo is minimized by the smallness of the tanks.

Tankers which carry lubricating or crude oil are fitted with internal heating systems to keep the cargo at the right temperature, otherwise it might have to be dug out instead of being pumped out. The danger of fire is less with this type of oil, but petrol and other highly inflammable spirits require careful handling.

During the 1960s new tankers have grown larger and larger, so that the vessel of 30,000 tons dwt. has become almost commonplace and many ships have surpassed 750 ft. in length and a gross tonnage of 30,000. Even larger tankers are building and the first to exceed 100,000 tons dwt. was the *Universe Apollo*, 72,133 g.t., 949 ft. o.a., built in Japan for Liberian owners. It is more economical to carry cargoes in these monster tankers but facilities at terminal ports will limit their routes; they will be unable to pass through the Suez Canal with a full load. Tankers of 500,000 tons dwt. are now discussed.

In addition to great increase in size other changes are prominent in tanker design. Some of the latest vessels have no separate bridge (*see* Plate XI, upper) and others have a new type of tower navigating bridge which rises well above the after superstructure.

COASTAL TANKER
(Plate XXXI)

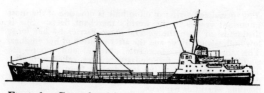

Fig. 26. Coastal spirit tanker. This 10-knot vessel was built in 1960 and is powered by a turbo-charged diesel. She has a length of 230 ft. o.a. and 1,570 tons dwt. capacity.

THE coastal tanker is a smaller version of the ocean-going tanker. Her trips are usually short and she may be employed for many months, or years, on the same route between ports only a few sailing hours apart. The ocean-going tanker discharges her cargo at large oil installations or refineries (such as Fawley near Southampton), and fleets of coastal tankers distribute the oil or petrol to smaller depots.

The coastal tanker generally has her navigating bridge on the poop, leaving a clear space between the poop and the forecastle. The tank top in this space is at two levels; the centre section is a few feet higher, forming what is known as a trunk deck. The lower level on each side is only a few inches above the waterline when the vessel is carrying a full cargo. The single mast may carry one light derrick for loading stores or the hoses.

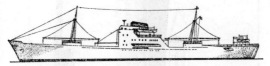

FIG. 27. Danish fast fruit carrier, 4,762 g.t., 434 ft. o.a., speed 19¼ knots.

THE refrigerated fruit ship is designed for the carriage of up to 1,800 tons of bananas, or other tropical fruit, kept at low temperatures in a large number of small compartments insulated by cork, wool or glass wool. The vessel is usually of medium size, but unlike a general cargo ship of comparable size she is capable of speeds up to 19 knots. Her attractive and almost yacht-like shape has a long forecastle, or continuous forecastle and poop; the hull is frequently painted white The routes are: West Indies–Europe, Caribbean–New York, California–Europe.

The refrigerated meat ship is employed on longer voyages, between Australia, New Zealand or the River Plate and the U.K., and is generally a much larger vessel than the fruit ship, carrying general cargo as well as chilled and frozen meat cargoes. Some of these ships also carry passengers and are classed as cargo-passenger liners.

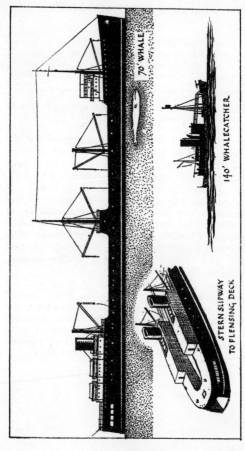

70' WHALE

140' WHALECATCHER

STERN SLIPWAY
TO FLENSING DECK

FIG. 28.   Whale oil factory ship

WHALE FACTORY SHIP
(Plate XXXI)

THE appearance of the standard type whale factory ship resembles that of a large tanker, but the bridge is usually further forward and she has a higher freeboard, heavy derricks and kingposts and evidence of more crew accommodation. Her main feature is a stern slipway through which the whales are hauled up to the flensing deck. Some vessels have twin funnels, like the train or car ferry, in order to allow a clear way for this entrance to the upper working deck.

Russian, Norwegian, Dutch and Japanese whale factories leave their home ports in October and spend the whole of the Antarctic summer in the whaling grounds, returning home in the early spring. The whales are harpooned from small, fast catchers (*see* page 159) attached to the "mother" ship. The carcasses are hauled up on to the flensing deck, cut up and the parts disposed of in the form of blubber, oil, meat and other by-products. These products are sometimes brought back to Europe during the whaling season by attendant ships which keep the mother ship supplied with fuel oil and other necessities.

One of the latest and largest whale factories is a 36,000 g.t. Russian vessel propelled by two powerful diesels. This ship is capable of dealing with 4,000 whales each trip and has accommodation for 650 crew and processing plant workers. Whale factories are equipped with the latest electronic devices and some have a helicopter, or amphibian aircraft, for spotting the whales. The last British whale factory was disposed of in 1963. The illustration opposite shows an older type of vessel but the main features are indicated. A recent Russian combination whaling/fish factory ship has a large single funnel and much longer and larger bridge superstructure forward.

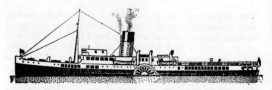

Fig. 29. An excursion paddle steamer built in 1937, length 200 ft., 600 g.t., operating in the summer in the Bournemouth area

THE excursion, or ferry, paddle steamer is the only survivor of the numerous early nineteenth-century vessels with this type of propulsion. The side paddles allow the vessel to make quick turns and rapid manœuvres alongside piers, particularly in strong currents. This advantage can now be obtained, however, by the Voith-Schneider type of propeller which gives great manœuvrability (*see* page 73).

The paddle steamer is distinctive in appearance with her long, light superstructure, one or two raked masts without derricks, and paddle boxes. The clear deck spaces and large public rooms allow the paddle ship to accommodate as many as 2,000 passengers on day excursions in sheltered waters.

Each year the British paddle fleet diminishes in size as the ships are either replaced by modern screw ships on the ferry services (such as the Portsmouth–Isle of Wight route) or taken off the uneconomic services from seaside resorts. In a few years the type will have vanished altogether. For this reason the Paddle Steamer Preservation Society has been formed, and this group of enthusiasts has acquired a 1923 example of this interesting and attractive ship.

POWER YACHTS

As a rule the term "yacht" is applied to almost any type of pleasure vessel whether she is propelled by sail, steam or diesel. The large luxury yacht is expensive to buy and to maintain. Numerous in the early part of the century, the graceful steam yachts (a) have been replaced by the low sleek motor yacht (d), smaller in size and more economical to run. Since the war many ex-*Fairmile* naval launches (b) have been converted for private use and many are also employed on public services such as the summer runs between Poole, Bournemouth and Swanage and services in the Channel Islands.

The Pilot Cutter is a yacht-like vessel which may be mistaken for a pleasure craft although she usually has large letters or numerals painted on her topsides. She has accommodation for a number of pilots and her duty is to lie off the entrance to a large port—such as the Thames or Mersey—to supply pilots for the incoming ships and take on board those who are leaving their outgoing ones. One of the latest British pilot boats is the *Edmund Gardner*, built for the Mersey Docks and Harbour Board. She is a diesel-electric vessel with a length of 165 ft. o.a., a speed of just over 13 knots and accommodation for 32 pilots. The drawing (c) shows a Belgian vessel of the same type.

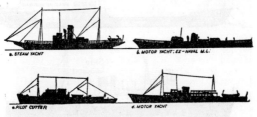

FIG. 30. Power yachts

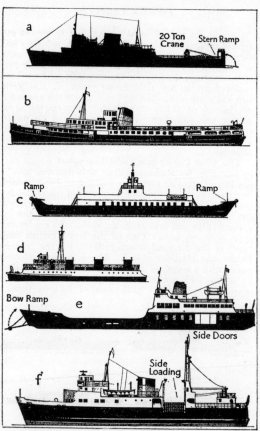

FIG. 31. Passenger and vehicle ferries

PASSENGER AND VEHICLE FERRIES

ESTUARIAL ferries vary a good deal in size and appearance. Cars may be loaded by either bow or stern ramps, or both, or by side doors according to the convenience at the terminal ports. During recent years a number of experimental craft have been built.

(a) The *Bardic Ferry* is the first merchant ship designed for what is now called the "roll-on, roll-off" type of service mainly for commercial vehicles. She belongs to a company operating such services between England, Ireland and the Continent. The vehicles are loaded by a stern ramp to the lower deck and by a 20-ton crane to the upper deck. She has cabin accommodation for 53 persons, a length of 338 ft. and 2,700 g.t.

(b) *Mountwood* is a modern diesel ferry operating across the River Mersey between Liverpool and Birkenhead carrying 1,200 passengers only.

(c) *Freshwater* is a double-ended ferry for passengers, mail, baggage, cars and cattle between Lymington and Yarmouth (Isle of Wight). She is fitted with two Voith-Schneider propellers placed at diagonally opposite corners of the hull. Built in 1960, 164 ft. o.a., 350 g.t., $10\frac{1}{2}$ knots.

(d) Tilbury–Gravesend ferry for 475 passengers. Six hydraulically operated side gangways. Voith-Schneider propeller. 110 ft. o.a.

(e) *Carisbrooke Castle*. Built in 1959, this twin-screw, dual-purpose ship can carry either 1,200 passengers and no cars, or 450 passengers and up to 45 vehicles between Southampton and Cowes (Isle of Wight). Side loading is provided but main loading is by a bow ramp similar to that of the converted wartime landing craft which preceded her on this service. Diesel engines, 14 knots, 191 ft. o.a., 672 g.t.

(f) The *Cowal* is a twin-screw passenger and car ferry running between Gourock and Dunoon and the Firth of Clyde. She has side loading, and accommodation for 34 cars. 186 ft. o.a., 569 g.t. Built 1954.

A very fine example of the car ferry is the *Free Enterprise*, a 2,500-ton vessel built in 1962 for the Dover–Calais route. She has two squat funnels placed athwartships and a handsome profile.

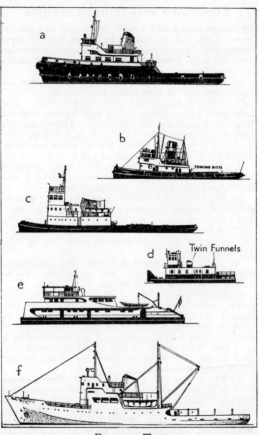

FIG. 32.   Tugs

THE TUG

ALTHOUGH they vary a good deal in size, tugs cannot be mistaken for any other type of ship. The super-structure is comparatively high, and placed well for-ward, leaving a clear flat deck space aft over which the steel hoops protect the deck fittings from the tow rope. The latter is attached to the towing hook, or bitts, at the after end of the superstructure.

(a) *Gatcombe*. 1960. 512 g.t., 136 ft. o.a., 12½ knots, 1,800 b.h.p. This twin-screw tug/tender was built for towing purposes in Southampton Water and for the conveyance of 400 passengers (or six cars and half that number of passengers) between Southampton Docks and liners which do not proceed up to the port itself but lie off the Isle of Wight.

(b) *Canning*. 1954. 200 g.t., 92 ft., 1,100 b.h.p. This tug manœuvres ocean-going merchant ships in and out of Liverpool Docks and the Mersey.

(c) *Stackgarth*. 1959. 306 g.t., 127 ft., 12 knots, 1,300 b.h.p. Built for the new Milford Haven oil terminal, this diesel tug is also equipped for fire-fight-ing and is able to deliver water at the rate of 3,000 gallons per minute.

(d) *Myrtle Lee*. 1959. 64 ft., 290 b.h.p. Kort nozzles. In North America the tug is called a tow-boat and it is usual for it to push ships rather than tow them. The drawing shows a small pusher tow-boat built for work on the Tennessee River.

(e) *Olivier van Noort*. 1959. 119 ft., 750 h.p. Push boats are also employed on the River Rhine. The twin-screw motor tug is capable of pushing four 1,500-ton barges upstream and she is fitted with six rudders and Kort nozzle units.

(f) *Herkules*. 1961. 3,500 b.h.p. The largest type of tug is the powerful ocean-going salvage vessel equipped to deal with disasters far out at sea. The *Herkules* is a Norwegian ship built for long-distance towing (based on Gibraltar) and also for icebreaking work during the winter in Scandinavia.

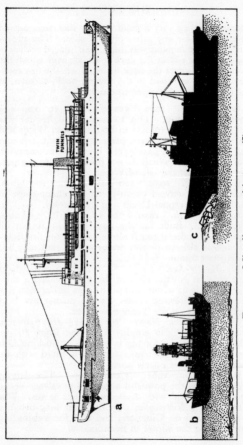

TWIN
FUNNELS

a

b   c

Fig. 33. Miscellaneous ship types (I)

76

MISCELLANEOUS TYPES

(a) CABLE SHIP

Most cable ships are owned by post office and telegraph companies. The clipper bows are characteristic. The sheaves fitted in the bows and stern are pulleys over which the cable runs either out over the stern when laying new cable or over the bows when repairing. New cable is stowed in large vertical cylinders. The cable ship is fitted with electrical detection apparatus, powerful winches and efficient workshops. The illustration (a) shows *Mercury*, 8,000 g.t., with a length of 473 ft. o.a. and a speed of 16½ knots. She entered service in 1963 for cable laying in the Pacific.

(b) LIGHTSHIP. British type.

In this country, the lightship is non-self-propelling and is towed to her station by a tug or lighthouse tender. In some countries the lightship has propelling machinery to ease the strain on the cables by going ahead on the engines. The modern ship is well equipped with all the latest apparatus for radio, sound signalling and radio direction transmitters.

Some lightships are unmanned and the apparatus is automatic. Lighthouse service tenders pay periodic visits to replenish gas cylinders and adjust machinery.

In England and Scotland lightships are painted red, and in Ireland they are black. The name of the station is painted in large white letters on each side of the hull, for example: SUNK in the Thames, NORTH CARR in the Firth of Forth and SHAMBLES near Portland Bill.

(c) ICEBREAKER

The icebreaker is required wherever ice is a handicap to shipping, as in the Baltic and certain North American ports. She is usually diesel-electrically operated. The fore part of the hull is strengthened and is shaped so that the vessel rides up on the ice and her weight crushes and breaks it. The drawing shows a British-built vessel of 160 ft. owned by the Polish Government. The Russian *Lenin* (1957) is propelled by turbo-electric machinery and nuclear reactors.

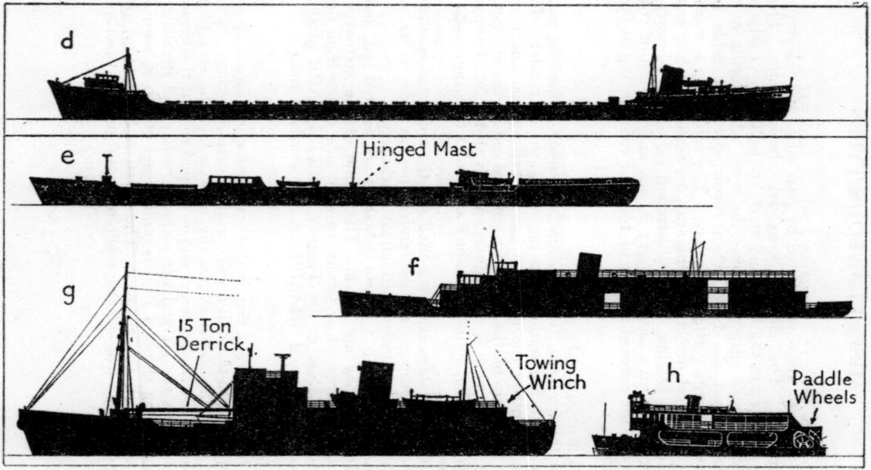

Paddle Wheels

Towing Winch

Hinged Mast

15 Ton Derrick

d

e

f

g

h

FIG. 34. Miscellaneous ship types (II)

(d) GREAT LAKES ORE CARRIER. 1959. 17,000 g.t. 715 ft. o.a. 16 knots.

This type of bulk carrier is built for the special conditions of the trade in the Great Lakes where the terminal ports are fully equipped with the necessary loading and discharging gear; thus the carrier has no need for such equipment. The forward position of the bridge is one of the characteristic features, and sometimes she has a tall boom rising from the stem to assist the helmsman.

(e) FLATIRON COLLIER. 1947. 1,773 g.t. 261 ft.

Built to carry coal to the up-river Thames power stations and gas works, the "flattie" has an unusually low superstructure and the masts and radar poles are hinged, or telescopic, so that they can be lowered under the many London bridges. The old type steam flatiron had a hinged funnel but the modern motorship has a funnel exhaust which is low enough for the bridges.

(f) HOSPITAL SHIP (see also page 123). 1959. 212 ft. 10 knots.

This twin-screw vessel is a shallow draught diesel ship used for carrying invalids on sightseeing tours through the inland waterways of Holland. She is fitted with 70 beds and accommodation for doctors and nurses.

(g) LIGHTHOUSE TENDER. 1960. 1,425 g.t. 221 ft. o.a. 13 knots.

This ship, and others owned by Trinity House and the Scottish Commissioners of Northern Lights, is employed in servicing lightships, lighthouses and light buoys and for conveying stores and keepers to them. She has accommodation for 21 light officers and lightsmen, a powerful winch aft (for towing lightships) and a heavy derrick forward for hoisting the buoys out of the water. Anchors and buoys can also be lifted forward by cables passing through the sheaves in the stem. (See also Cable Ship, page 77.)

(h) RIVER PASSENGER VESSEL. 100 ft. 67 g.t.

On most of the world's large rivers there are passenger vessels with shallow draught and a long, high superstructure such as the one shown here. She is a diesel ship employed by the Sudan Government Railways carrying passengers on the River Nile, and is propelled by a paddle wheel on each quarter.

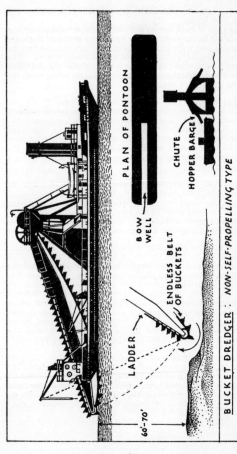

PLAN OF PONTOON

BOW WELL

CHUTE

HOPPER BARGE

ENDLESS BELT OF BUCKETS

LADDER

60'-70'

BUCKET DREDGER : *NON-SELF-PROPELLING TYPE*

FIG. 35.   Bow well non-self-propelled bucket ladder dredger

HARBOUR CRAFT

BUCKET LADDER DREDGER

DREDGING operations are carried on whenever it is necessary to maintain the depth of water in channels, docks and basins. The spoil is dredged from the bottom and must be removed to dumping grounds some distance out at sea. Some vessels which have hopper space and are self-propelled can take the spoil to the dumping grounds, but as the bucket dredger has no hopper space and is not self-propelled it is moved about the port by tugs and transfers the spoil to hopper barges.

The hull shape of the dredger is peculiar. It has a well in the centre so that the bucket ladder can be lowered to a maximum depth of about 70 ft., which is sometimes necessary where there is a wide tidal range. The well can be in the bows, in the centre or at the stern. The last arrangement gives a more seaworthy hull.

The ladder has an endless belt of buckets each with a capacity of between 20 and 25 cu. ft. The belt moves round, and as each bucket reaches the bottom it scoops up the spoil and carries it to the top of the ladder, where a tripping device tips the bucket and empties the spoil down a chute into the hopper barge. A normal-sized dredger is able to move about 1,000 cubic feet of spoil per hour. The machinery is driven by reciprocating steam engines situated near the stern.

A new Dutch diesel-propelled hopper-dredger (312 ft. o.a.) appears much more like an engines aft freighter. A powerful suction tube replaces the bucket ladder and the hopper space is discharged by pumps instead of gravity. The traditional type of bucket dredger is likely to be replaced by the trailing suction dredger, which is more mobile and more economical.

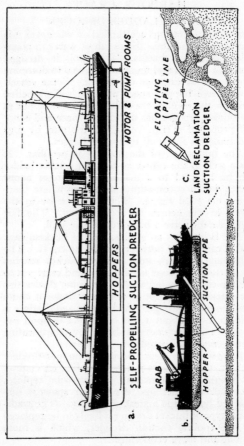

MOTOR & PUMP ROOMS

HOPPERS

SELF-PROPELLING SUCTION DREDGER

a.

FLOATING
PIPELINE

c.
LAND RECLAMATION
SUCTION DREDGER

GRAB

SUCTION PIPE

HOPPER

b.

FIG. 36. Suction dredgers

82

SUCTION DREDGER

THE suction dredger, also known as a sand-pump or hydraulic dredger, is required when the bottom is mainly sand. A pipe is lowered to the bottom and the spoil, perhaps three-quarters of it water, is drawn up into the hoppers. The nozzle at the end of the suction pipe is sometimes fitted with a revolving cutter to break up certain grounds; sometimes a strong jet of water is played on the bottom for the same purpose.

Fig. 36a shows a powerful vessel nearly 300 ft. long and over 4,000 tons' displacement. She has diesel engines giving her a speed of 12 knots. Some American dredgers of this type are 500 ft. long and are very ship-like. Diesel-electric suction dredgers may be seen working off the Needles (Isle of Wight), where they dredge aggregate from the sea bed. They resemble coasters but may be distinguished by the large horizontal pipe between the forecastle and poop.

The second drawing (b) shows an unusual suction dredger which also has a grab, and hopper arrangements similar to those of an ordinary dumb hopper (*see* Fig. 40).

Another type of suction dredger is the land reclamation dredger (c). She is far from being ship-like, and is usually just a rectangular pontoon bearing the pumping machinery and sheerlegs for lifting and lowering the suction pipe. The spoil can either be transferred to a hopper alongside or carried by a floating pipeline to the area which is being reclaimed.

FIG. 37. Motor lifeboat of the Royal National Lifeboat Institution

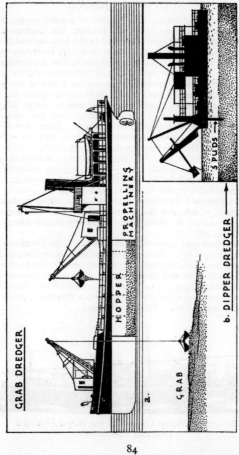

FIG. 38. Self-propelling grab hopper and dipper dredgers

GRAB DREDGER

In its simplest form the grab dredger is a pontoon with a slewing and hoisting crane capable of operating a double-chain grab. Many improvised craft are like this, while others have a seaworthy hull with a hopper and four grab cranes and self-propelling machinery. The grab dredger has the advantage of being able to work in awkward corners of docks and basins. Like the other types of dredger, it may transfer its spoil into hoppers which are towed to sea by tugs.

The dredger illustrated in Fig. 38a is 150 ft. overall length, and is just over 400 tons.

The dipper dredger is popular in the Far East, but is not often seen in Europe. It is a large pontoon with steam machinery at one end and a heavy crane with dipper gear at the other.

The important part of the dipper gear is the shovel, which may have a capacity of 40 cu. ft. This shovel is lowered into the water and the spoil conveyed to a hopper; its action is exactly like that of the land excavator. This dredger has no hopper space and no propelling machinery. It has legs, called *spuds*, which are lowered to the bottom to prevent movement while dredging is in progress.

Fig. 38b shows such a dredger fitted with awnings and covered decks for service in hot countries.

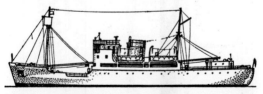

Fig. 39. The diesel-electric royal research ship *John Biscoe*. 1,584 g.t. 220 ft. Completed in 1956

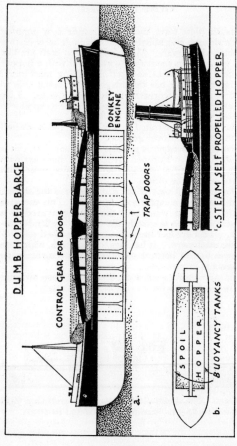

FIG. 40. Hopper barges

HOPPER BARGES

The non-self-propelling or dumb Hopper Barge is the "maid of all work" for all dredgers not fitted with holds for their spoil. It is a large open barge between 100 and 200 ft. in length. The forecastle has space for stores and crew, and at the after end is machinery for operating the hopper doors in the bottom of the vessel. These doors occupy the whole bottom of the hopper space and are controlled by chains which pass over pulleys in the fore-and-aft girder to the machinery aft. When the doors are opened the heavier-than-water spoil falls out and is deposited on the sea bottom while the water remains in the hopper, which is fitted with buoyancy tanks. That is why a hopper returning from the dumping grounds is still apparently fully loaded.

The curved girder mentioned above is the hopper's most distinctive feature as it spans the space between the forecastle and poop. A dumb hopper barge may have a small funnel from the donkey engine boiler, and sometimes has a small bridge and wheelhouse.

The self-propelling hopper barge has the same features as the dumb hopper, but with a longer poop, a large funnel and more prominent bridge.

As the dumping grounds are usually several miles out to sea both types must be seaworthy.

BARGE

The cargo-carrying barge, like the hopper barge, is either "dumb" or self-propelling. The subdivision of the hull follows the same arrangement as in the hopper barge, but the hopper space is replaced by a large clear cargo hold. Barges (known in some places as *lighters*) vary a good deal in size, from the huge steel Rhine barges, able to carry about 1,000 tons of cargo, to the small English canal boat. The latter is known as a *narrow boat* as its beam is not more than seven feet. The nomadic boatman and his family live on board and take a great pride in their floating home, which is sometimes gaily painted with traditional decorations.

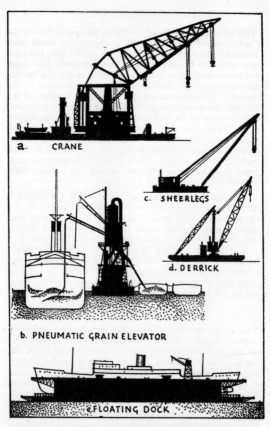

a. CRANE

c. SHEERLEGS

b. PNEUMATIC GRAIN ELEVATOR

d. DERRICK

e. FLOATING DOCK

FIG. 41.   Harbour craft

FLOATING HARBOUR APPLIANCES

THE FLOATING CRANE (a) is conspicuous in most of our large ports, where its jib towers over the surrounding sheds and warehouses. It handles heavy lifts such as lock gates, boilers and other unusually bulky pieces of dock machinery within the dock area. Some floating cranes handle ordinary cargoes.

The floating crane is nearly always self-propelling. The Port of London Authority has 60-ton cranes fitted with Voith–Schneider propellers giving high manœuvrability. The hoisting of the load, and the various actions of the crane are usually run by electricity from generators driven by steam engines, which also propel the crane.

Some of the largest floating cranes are able to lift up to 350 tons on a short jib radius and 250 tons on a longer radius. The pontoon has many watertight compartments for stability when the crane is at work.

THE FLOATING DERRICK (d) is a normal derrick type of crane on a non-self-propelling pontoon.

THE FLOATING SHEERLEGS (c) is used for extremely heavy lifts over short distances within the port.

THE FLOATING PNEUMATIC GRAIN ELEVATOR (b) is common in many ports. It not only discharges grain from a ship's hold at high speed but also sacks and weighs it before depositing it either into barges alongside or on to conveyor belts to the grain warehouse. The pumps and other auxiliaries are usually worked by electricity from dock installations or from diesel-driven generators on the elevator.

THE FLOATING DOCK (e) depends on local conditions. When it is impossible or uneconomic to excavate dry docks, the floating dock serves the same purpose. The simplest type is a large pontoon with long side walls and open ends. Water is flooded into tanks in the pontoon to submerge the dock. To raise it again the water is pumped out. The largest extend 1,000 ft. and can lift ships of 60,000 or 70,000 tons.

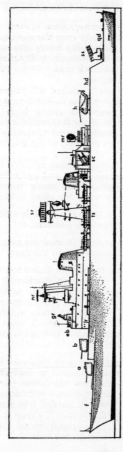

FIG. 42. A modern warship: *County* class guided missile destroyer (Plate XV). a and b. 4·5-in. radar controlled fully automatic dual-purpose quick-firing guns in twin turrets; eb. enclosed bridge; f. forecastle; lr. inflatable life rafts; gr. gun control radar; nr. search radar; sr. air warning search radar; ts. homing anti-submarine torpedo tubes; sc. Seacat close-range anti-aircraft missiles; mr. missile guidance radar; h. Westland Wessex "hunter killer" helicopter; hd. helicopter deck; qd. quarter deck; ss. Seaslug medium range missile launcher

4 — WARSHIPS
GENERAL CHARACTERISTICS

COLOUR. In all countries naval vessels are painted grey. Ships of the Royal Navy are painted a light grey with white topmasts if they are in commission; in reserve, the topmasts are painted grey. On service in certain Middle East areas the ships are painted white. All British submarines are painted black.

GENERAL APPEARANCE. The warship's long, low outline is broken by gun houses and controls, with the main superstructure building up around the foremast. This mast, and other projections, has a number of radar antennae and aerials, and unlike the cargo ship the warship never has a high stern or poop deck. She is generally flushed decked and may have a long forecastle deck which extends well aft.

PROPULSION. Most warships are propelled by high pressure steam turbines and oil-fired water-tube boilers. Although common for merchant ships, diesel motors are much less used for warships. Some recent frigates are fitted with diesels and they are used for some classes of fast patrol boats. Gas turbines have been introduced in the new *Tribal* class frigates and guided missile destroyers, not as main power units but as boosters to give extra power for high speeds. Nuclear powered submarines have been operational for some years, and the U.S. Navy cruiser *Long Beach* is the first surface warship to be propelled by turbines for which the steam is produced by nuclear reactors.

PROTECTION. The now obsolete battleship was protected amidships by armour plating up to sixteen inches in thickness, but the average armour now used for cruisers and carriers is not more than three or four inches thick for the ships' sides, and about two inches for the deck plating. Fleet escorts, destroyers and frigates have no armour plating at all.

SUBDIVISION OF THE HULL. Another difference (although not a visible one) between the cargo ship and the warship is that the hull of the former is divided into six to eight large compartments by watertight transverse bulkheads. On the other hand, the warship, with no large cargo hold requirements, is divided by many transverse and longitudinal watertight bulkheads into a great number of compartments which can be sealed off by watertight doors if there has been flooding through accident or naval action. Small warships do not have longitudinal bulkheads but they are nevertheless divided into a large number of compartments by numerous transverse bulkheads.

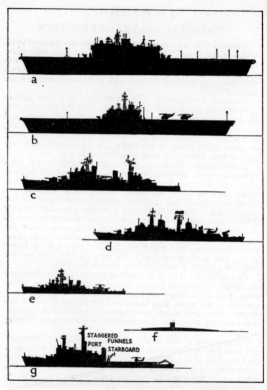

FIG. 43. Comparative silhouettes of British warships (I)

COMPARATIVE SILHOUETTES OF BRITISH WARSHIPS
(Fig. 43)

No.	Type and class of ship Date of building and major refit	Standard tonnage	Length o.a. (ft.)	Sea speed (knots)	Armament and aircraft	Pge ref.
a	Aircraft carrier *Eagle* 1952 (1964)*	44,100	803½	31·5	58 40-mm. A.A. Seacat g.m. 42+ aircraft	99
b	Aircraft carrier, light fleet and commando types 1954 (1960–62)	22,000	737½	28	40-mm. A.A. 21 aircraft **or** 16 helicopters	99
c	Cruiser *Tiger* class 1959–61	9,550	555½	31·5	2 6-in. (twin) 6 3-in. (twin)	101
d	Guided missile armed destroyer *County* class 1962	5,200	520½	32·5	4 4·5-in. (twin) 1 Seaslug 2 Seacats	90 105
e	*Tribal* class frigate 1961–63	2,300	360	28	2 4·5-in. 2 40-mm. A.A. 1 Limbo 1 helicopter	109
f	*Dreadnought* class submarine 1962. Nuclear powered	3,000	265¾	30	6 21-in. tubes (homing)	111
g	Assault landing ship *Fearless* class 1965	7,500	520	20	4 Seacats Helicopters	—

* Note. The dates in brackets refer to the latest large-scale re-fit.

BATTLESHIP

Over sixty years ago the famous *Dreadnought* revolutionized the design of the battleship and set the pattern for the most important units of the world's navies. Heavily armoured and equipped with up to ten guns of 14- or 16-in. calibre, these battleships dominated sea power for half a century. Now, however, the battleship's days are over and, with the development of the fast jet aircraft and guided missile replacing the big gun, the aircraft carrier has taken its place as the largest and most effective unit of a fleet.

FIG. 45. *King George V* class battleship

H.M.S. *Vanguard* was the last British battleship. Larger than the *King George V* class, she was scrapped in 1961 after a period as H.Q. ship at Portsmouth. The United States Navy has a few battleships in reserve but they are unlikely to become operational again. The 35,000-ton *North Carolina*, built in 1937, has been preserved as a war memorial at Wilmington, North Carolina.

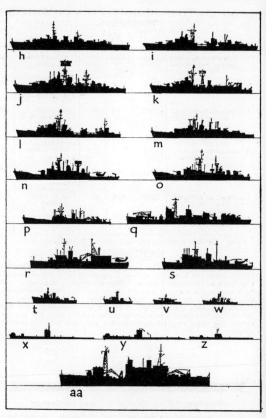

FIG. 44.   Comparative silhouettes of British warships
(II)

No.	Type, class, date of building and major refit (in brackets)	Standard tonnage	Length o.a. (ft.)	Sea speed (knots)	Armament and aircraft	Page ref.
h	Mine countermeasures support ship *Manxman* 1941 (1963)	3,000	418	37	4 40-mm. A.A.	121
i	Destroyer *Daring* class 1945–48	2,800	390	30·5	6 4·5-in. (twin) 4–6 40-mm. A.A. 5 21-in. tubes Seacat and Squid	107
j	Fleet radar picket *Battle* class 1943 (1962)	2,480	379	30·5	4 4·5-in. (twin) Seacat and Squid	109
k	Fleet radar picket *Weapon* class 1944 (1959)	2,280	365	30·75	4 4-in. 6 40-mm. A.A. Limbo or Squid	109
l	Fast anti-submarine frigate T class 1943 (1952)	1,810	363	31·25	2 4-in. (twin) 7 40-mm. A.A. 4 21-in. tubes Squid	109
m	Fast anti-submarine frigate R class 1943 (1949–51)	2,030	358	31·25	2 4-in. (twin) 2 40-mm. A.A. Limbo and Squid	109
n	General purpose frigate *Leander* class 1961–62	2,200	372	30	2 4·5-in. (twin) Seacat Helicopter with homing torpedoes	109
o	Anti-aircraft frigate *Leopard* class 1957–59	2,300	340	25 (Diesel)	4 4·5-in. (twin) 2 40-mm. A.A. Squid	109
p	Anti-aircraft frigate *Blackwood* class 1956–59	1,180	310	24·5	3 40-mm. A.A. 4 21-in. tubes Limbo	109
q	Escort maintenance ship *Hartland Point* 1945 (1960)	8,580	441	11	11 40-mm.	119
r	Ice patrol ship 1936 (1955)	3,450	338	20	2 40-mm. 4 20-mm. 2 helicopters	
s	Survey ship *Vidal* 1940 (1962)	1,940	315	15	4 3-pounders 1 helicopter	121
t	Coastal minesweeper *Ton* class 1953	360	153	15	1 40-mm. A.A. 2 20-mm.	113
u	Inshore minesweeper *Ham* class 1952+	120	106	14	1 40-mm. A.A.	113
v	Fast patrol boat *Brave* class 1960	89	99	50 Gas turbine	Gunboat: 2 40-mm. 2 21-in. tubes Torpedo boat: 4 21-in. tubes 1 40-mm.	115

w	Seaward defence boat Ford class 1956+	120	117	15	1 40-mm. A.A Squid	115
x	Attack submarine Oberon class 1960–62	1,610	295	25	8 21-in. homing torpedoes	111
y	Submarine A class 1945–48	1,120	282	19 (8)	1 4-in. 8 21-in. tubes or mines	111
z	Fast experimental submarine Ex class 1956–58	780	225	25 submerged		111

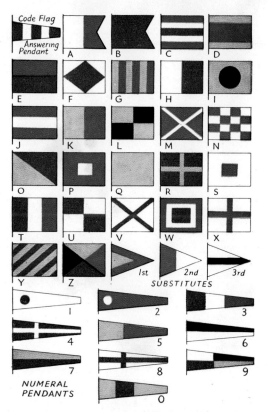

PLATE I.—International Code flags (*see* p. 20)

PLATE II.—Cunard passenger liner *Caronia* in New York harbour (*see* p. 45)

Upper and lower photographs by A. Duncan; middle photograph by courtesy of Ben Line Ltd.

PLATE III.—Fast cargo liners (*see* p. 51)
Upper: Clan Macnair
Middle: Benarty
Lower: City of Newcastle

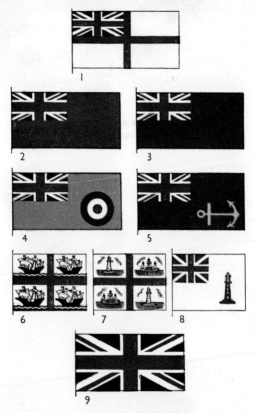

PLATE IV.—British flags and ensigns (*see* p. 23)

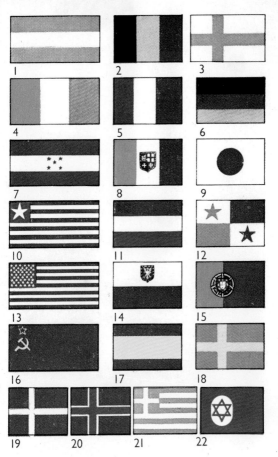

PLATE V.—Merchant flags (*see* p. 25)

PLATE VI.—Coasters (I) (*see* p. 59)
Upper: Collier *Branksome*
Lower: General trader *Security*

Lower photograph by A. Duncan
PLATE VII.—Coasters (II) (*see* p. 59)
Upper: Loch Ard
Lower: Sherborne

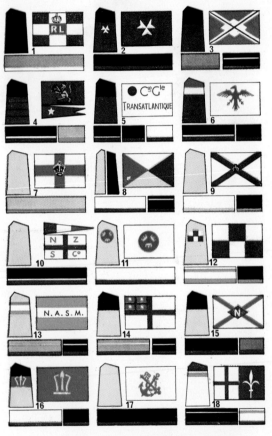

PLATE VIII.—Colours of shipping companies
Passenger liners (*see* p. 26)

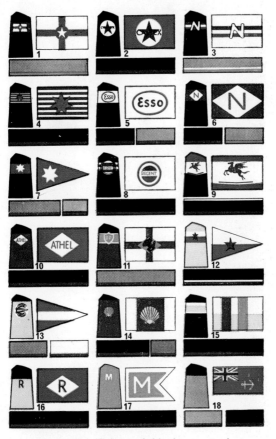

PLATE IX.—Colours of shipping companies
Tankers (*see* p. 28)

Upper photograph by courtesy of British Railways, Southern Region; lower photograph by courtesy of Thoresen Car Ferries

PLATE X.—Cross-Channel ships (*see* pp. 61 and 63)

Upper: Train ferry *Saint Germain*
Lower: Car ferry *Viking*

Both photographs reproduced by courtesy of the British Petroleum Co. Ltd.

PLATE XI.—Tankers (*see* p. 65)
Upper: British Mariner
Lower: British Queen

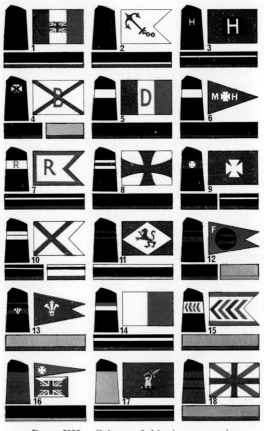

PLATE XII.—Colours of shipping companies
British oceangoing freighters and passenger/cargo
liners (I) (see p. 30)

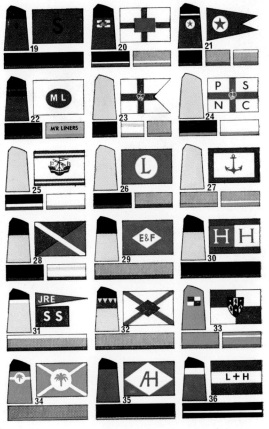

PLATE XIII.—Colours of shipping companies
British oceangoing freighters and passenger/cargo
liners (II) (*see* p. 31)

Both photographs Crown copyright

PLATE XIV.—British warships (I)
Upper: Cruiser H.M.S. *Lion* (*see* p. 101)
Lower: Nuclear submarine H.M.S. *Dreadnought*
(*see* p. 111)

All photographs Crown copyright
PLATE XV.—British warships (II)
Upper: Guided missile ship H.M.S. *Devonshire*
(*see* p. 105)
Middle: Guided missile ship H.M.S. *Kent* (*see* p. 105)
Lower: Frigate H.M.S. *Leander* (*see* p. 95)

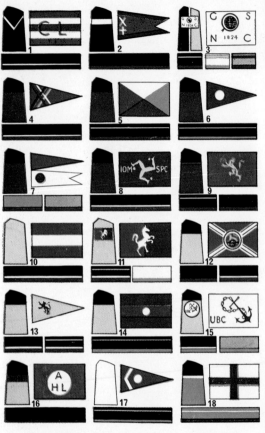

PLATE XVI.—Colours of shipping companies
British short sea passenger, cargo and excursion
services (*see* p. 33)

PLATE XVII.—Colours of shipping companies
Coastal and short sea cargo ships (*see* p. 35)

PLATE XVIII.—Aircraft carriers (*see* p. 99)
Upper: H.M.S. *Ark Royal*
Lower: U.S.S. *Forrestal*

*Upper and middle, official U.S. Navy photographs; lower photograph
by Skyfotos*

PLATE XIX.—Cruisers (*see* pp. 101 and 103)
Upper: U.S.S. *Springfield*
Middle: U.S.S. *Northampton*
Lower: Russian *Sverdlov*

PLATE XX.—Union-Castle passenger liner *Pretoria Castle* (see p. 47)

By courtesy of P. & O.-Orient Line

PLATE XXI.—P. & O.-Orient passenger liner *Canberra* (see p. 49)

PLATE XXII.—Nuclear powered surface warships
Upper: U.S.S. *Bainbridge* (frigate) (*see* p. 105)
Middle: U.S.S. *Long Beach* (cruiser) (*see* p. 101)
Lower: U.S.S. *Enterprise* (aircraft carrier) (*see* p. 99)

All photographs by courtesy of the French Naval Attaché

PLATE XXIII.—French warships (*see* pp. 103, 107 and 109)

Upper: Cruiser *Colbert* (*see* p. 103)
Middle: Destroyer *Kersaint* (*see* p. 107)
Lower: Frigate *Le Corse* (*see* p. 109)

PLATE XXIV.—P. & O.-Orient passenger liner *Iberia* (see p. 47)

PLATE XXV.—Cross-Channel ship *Duke of Lancaster* (see p. 61)

Lower photograph by Skyfotos

PLATE XXVI.—Sail schoolships

Upper: French *La Belle Poule* (see p. 137)
Lower: Danish *Danmark* (see p. 131)

PLATE XXVII.—Rigging of *Cutty Sark* (*see* p. 129)

By courtesy of Cunard Line

PLATE XXVIII.—Cunard passenger/cruising liner *Mauretania* at Malta (*see* p. 45), also minesweeper (*see* p. 113)

PLATE XXIX.—Blue Funnel passenger/cargo liner *Centaur* at Port Said

Photographs by courtesy of British Trawlers' Federation
PLATE **XXX**.—Fishing vessels
Upper: Distant water trawler *Cape Canaveral* (see p. 155)
Lower: Stern trawler *Junella* (see p. 157)

All photographs by A. Duncan

PLATE XXXI.—*Upper:* Coastal tanker *Midhurst* (*see* p. 66)

Middle: Bulk carrier *Morar* (*see* p. 57)

Lower: Whale factory ship *Kyokuyo Maru* No. 3 (*see* p. 69)

PLATE XXXII.—British collier *Mendip* at Portsmouth

ARMAMENT OF BRITISH WARSHIPS

Calibre	Mounting, type or other characteristics	Types of warship
6 in.	Twin or triple mounting in armoured turrets. Recent guns fully automatic. 20 rounds per minute. Dual purpose; high and low angle.	Cruisers; main armament
4·5 in.	Single or twin mountings in armoured turrets, fully automatic and radar controlled. Dual purpose	Destroyers; main armament Large carriers Submarine depot ship Frigates Motor gun boats
4 in.	Single or twin mounting. Lightly armoured gunhouses. Anti-aircraft	Secondary armament of some cruisers Frigates
3 in.	Single or twin mounting. Armoured turrets. 120 rounds per minute	Secondary armament of new cruisers
40 mm.	Bofors. Mountings of one, two or six barrels. Open or light shields. High speed close range anti-aircraft guns. May be fully automatic and radar controlled.	Standard for most warships
20 mm.	Oerlikon, single mountings. Heavy machine guns	Minesweepers, secondary armament
4·85 ft. (length) 19·65 ft.	*Seacat* surface-to-air guided missile for close visual range anti-aircraft duty *Seaslug* surface-to-air guided missile for long range duty; 20 miles. Travels along ship's radar beam. Proximity fuse for near misses	Aircraft carriers, guided missile ships, destroyers and frigates *County* class guided missile destroyers
21 in.	Torpedo tubes. Single, triple or quadruple mountings; swivelling. New type homing torpedoes on fixed mountings	Few destroyers and frigates, but generally being removed from surface ships Anti-submarine frigates Shipborne helicopters Submarines; main armament Motor torpedo boats
	Anti-submarine mortar bombs Squid earlier type. Short range Limbo long barrels, triple launcher, automatic depth setting related to Asdic. Have replaced depth charges.	Destroyers and frigates Seaward defence boats

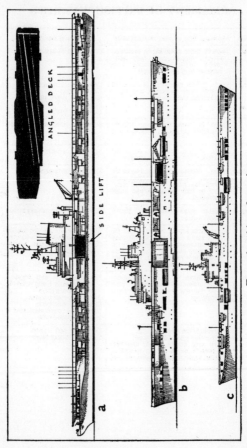

FIG. 46. Aircraft carriers

AIRCRAFT CARRIER
(Plate XVIII)

THE aircraft carrier is easily recognized by the immense flight deck, with neither camber nor sheer, which stretches the full length and width of the vessel. The funnel, control tower and navigating bridge form a narrow island super-structure on the starboard side. The carrier has no offen-sive guns but has a number of dual purpose 4- to 5-inch guns and numerous light A.A. guns for defence. Great endurance is coupled with high speed. The flight deck may be of three-inch plating and part of the hull streng-thened by armour plating to protect the machinery.

A British invention is found on most carriers. The flight line is set at an angle of between 5° and 8° so that an aircraft which is likely to overshoot can safely do so and make another touch down instead of flying into the crash barrier. Another British invention, the steam catapult, is in general use. Many new developments have been necessi-tated by the use of faster and heavier jet-propelled aircraft and new types of missile.

The largest operational carrier in the world is the U.S. *Enterprise*, 1,102 ft. in length, and with nuclear reactors providing the steam for her turbines she has a cruising range of about half a million miles without refuelling. She can carry over a hundred aircraft. With no need for funnel uptakes the bridge superstructure is unusually square and comparatively small. Her eight reactors will give her a speed of over 30 knots (Plate XXII).

For the first time since the war, a British aircraft carrier is to be laid down; she will be a 50,000-ton vessel propelled by conventional power and is expected to enter service in 1971.

Illustrations (Fig. 46)

(a) U.S. *Midway* class. 51,000 tons. 968 ft. o.a. 33 knots. Armament of 10 5-in. and 22 3-in. guns, and guided missiles. 137 aircraft. Built 1945-47.

(b) British *Ark Royal*. 43,340 tons. 808 ft. o.a. 31·5 knots. Armament 8 4·5-in. guns. 32 40-mm. A.A. 42 aircraft. Laid down 1943 and completed 1955.

(c) British carrier. 22,000 tons. 737 ft. o.a. 29·5 knots. Carriers of this class have been converted as "Commando" carriers with a complement of 16 helicopters. Ex-R.N. light carriers of 16,000 tons are now owned by the Netherlands, France, India, Canada and Australia.

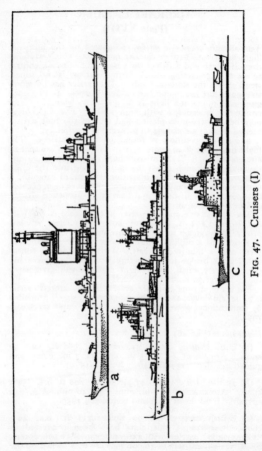

FIG. 47. Cruisers (I)

CRUISERS (I)
(Plate XIX)

THE cruiser is a general-purpose fighting vessel designed for high speed, endurance and comparatively heavy armament. Endurance is particularly important to British and United States cruisers in order to protect long trade routes all over the world. Some other navies have been able to pay less regard to this characteristic and develop faster ships. The largest cruisers now in operation are the U.S. 8-in. heavy cruisers such as the *Boston* class, one of the few survivors of the heavy class built by several nations in earlier years. The standard cruiser is now about 10,000 tons' displacement and armed with new type fully automatic 6-in. guns which are as effective as the early 8-in. guns.

A hybrid type of warship is under construction in France. She is a cruiser helicopter carrier, about 10,000 tons' displacement, with a speed of over 26 knots. She has a large bridge well forward, a helicopter deck aft and two single-mount 3–9-in. guns on a short quarter deck. Designed for war-time operations as a commando ship, helicopter carrier or troop transport, she will in peace-time be used for training purposes.

Illustrations (Fig. 47)

(a) U.S. cruiser *Long Beach*. 1961. 14,200 tons. 721 ft. o.a. 30·5 knots (Plate XXII). This, the first nuclear powered cruiser, is armed with guided missiles some of which are 31 ft. in length. Her silhouette is quite distinctive. No armour plating is fitted to this ship.

(b) R.N. *Tiger* class cruiser. 9,550 tons. 555½ ft. o.a. (Plate XIV). *Tiger*, *Lion* and *Blake* were laid down during the last war, launched 1944–45, but not completed until 1959–61. They were designed to give anti-aircraft support to carriers and merchant convoys as well as to assist in landings. With a speed of 31·5 knots they are armed with the latest fully automatic 6-in. guns in a twin turret in the forward and six rapid-firing 3-in. guns. The after 6-in. gun turret is now replaced by a flight deck and hangar for four helicopters. The vessels' sides are protected at the water line by a belt of 3¼-in. armour, and the turrets and deck have 2-in. plating. The conning tower is well protected with 4-in. armour.

(c) Italian *Doria* class. 6,000 tons. 483 ft. o.a. 30 knots. This class of cruiser is armed with eight 3-in. guns, guided missiles and torpedo tubes. Designed to act as escort cruisers or destroyer leaders, they also carry three helicopters for anti-submarine duty.

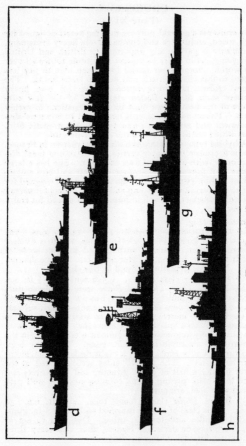

FIG. 48. Cruisers (II)

CRUSIERS (II)

Illustrations (Fig. 48)

(d) Netherlands *De Ruyter* class. 1953. 9,529 tons. 614 ft. o.a. Construction was started in 1939 but the two ships were not launched until 1953. They are equipped with fully automatic 6-in. guns and one ship has guided missile launchers. 32 knots.

(e) British *Belfast*. 1939. 11,550 tons. 613 ft. o.a. 30 knots. This improved *Southampton* class ship is the largest cruiser in the Royal Navy. She cannot be mistaken for any other warship with her distinctive arrangement of lattice mainmast between two sharply raked funnels. The twelve 6-in. guns are arranged in four triple turrets, two forward and two aft. The fifth British cruiser, *Sheffield*, has her mainmast aft of the second funnel. Since the war, some of the ex-R.N. *Colony* and *Dido* class light cruisers have found their way into Commonwealth and other navies.

(f) French *Colbert*. 1959. 8,720 tons. 597 ft. o.a. 32 knots (Plate XXIII). This cruiser is armed with eight twin-mounted 5-in. guns and a large number of anti-aircraft Bofors guns. In addition to duties as a cruiser she is fitted as a fleet command ship and could be used for the transport of 2,400 men with their gear and equipment. Her silhouette strikes a strong contrast with the untidier looking Dutch ship (d).

(g) Russian *Sverdlov* class. 1951 onwards. 15,450 tons. 689 ft. o.a. (Plate XIX). The ships in this large class have a designed speed of 34·5 knots and are equipped with twelve 6-in. guns in triple turrets. Some of the ships carry torpedo tubes and others a large number of mines; in some ships two of the gun turrets have been replaced by guided missile launchers.

(h) U.S. *Baltimore* class guided missile cruiser. 1943 (1955). 13,600 tons. 673 ft. o.a. 34 knots designed speed. Previously conventional 8-in. heavy cruisers, these ships have been converted for very efficient anti-aircraft duties. They are equipped with twin "Terrier" launchers (in place of X and Y gun turrets) which fire 27-ft. missiles with a speed of 1,500 m.p.h. against aircraft at long range. Two triple turrets containing 8-in. guns have been retained; other guns are 10 5-in. and 12 3-in., all on twin mountings. Other U.S. heavy cruisers are being similarly converted.

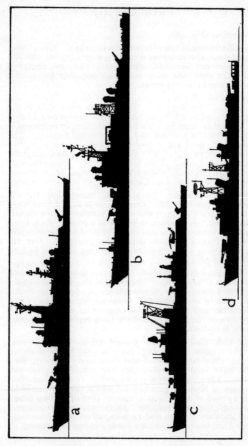

FIG. 49. Guided missile destroyers

GUIDED MISSILE DESTROYERS
(Plates XV and XXII)

THIS entirely new class of warship is generally referred to as a destroyer, but in size and striking power is much more like a light cruiser. Whereas the normal destroyer is designed to work with others in a flotilla, the new type of super-destroyer has sufficient armament, power and endurance to work alone. The drawing on page 90 shows the new British example of this class to be a powerful looking warship with clean lines. She is designed to give strong air defence to a large operational task force and also, by means of a helicopter and underwater detectors, to deal with enemy submarines. In the event of contamination by radio-active material she can be completely washed down. In addition to steam turbines she has gas turbines to supplement normal power for high speeds and to enable her to start quickly from "cold" in an emergency.

Illustrations (Fig. 49)

(a) Guided missile frigate, U.S., *Leahy* class. 1962. 5,670 tons. 535 ft. o.a. 34 knots. Armament 2 "Terrier" surface-to-air guided missile launchers and 2 3-in. guns. The funnel uptakes are incorporated in a solid-looking mast or tower.

(b) Nuclear powered guided missile frigate, U.S., *Bainbridge* class. 1962. 6,500 tons. 564 ft. o.a. 30 knots (Plate XXII). Armament 2 "Terrier" guided missiles, fore and aft, 2 3-in. guns, 6 torpedo tubes. This warship is the first destroyer type to be propelled by nuclear power, which will give many advantages. Her steaming range will be immense and the lack of funnels will make for better protection from fall-out, also the numerous radar antennae will not be affected by smoke and fumes.

(c) French light cruiser or destroyer leader. 1966. 4,400 tons. 518 ft. o.a. 34 knots. Armament surface-to-air guided missiles, 3·9-in. A.A. guns, rocket gliders that carry homing torpedoes for use against submarines. Homing torpedoes. One helicopter.

(d) Russian *Krupnyi* class guided missile destroyer. 1962–63. 3,500 tons. 453 ft. o.a. 38 knots. Surface-to-air guided missiles. 20 A.A. guns. Two triple torpedo mountings.

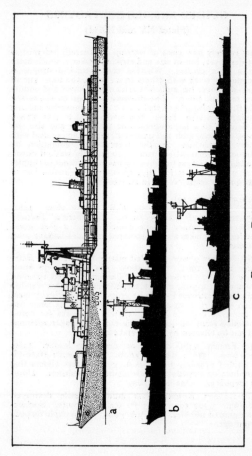

FIG. 50.   Destroyers

DESTROYER
(Plate XXIII)

THE destroyer is a small warship with a comparatively shallow draught; she is therefore able to visit many small ports and will consequently be more familiar than the larger warships. She is designed for high speed and good manœuvrability and has an all-purpose armament and no armour plating; her best defence is her speed and flexibility of movement. The destroyer may be armed with conventional guns, light A.A. weapons, mortars, torpedoes and guided missiles. In appearance she is long, low and sleek, often with a funnel which is incorporated in a lattice mast. Study of groups of destroyers of different countries shows that they do have quite distinct national characteristics. Apart from general duties some destroyers are fully equipped for specific work as radar pickets or anti-submarine ships.

The flotilla leader is a destroyer fitted to serve as the administrative headquarters ship for the flotilla; she is distinguished by a painted black band on the forward, or single, funnel.

Illustrations (Fig. 50)

(a) British *Daring* class destroyer. 1952–54. 2,800 tons. 390 ft. o.a. 30·5 knots. 6 4·5-in. guns in twin turrets, two forward and the others aft, 6 40-mm. A.A. guns, 5 21-in. torpedo tubes in one mounting. Seacat guided missiles and Squid triple-barrel mortar. The forward funnel is within the lattice foremast and the after funnel is quite diminutive. The guided missile launcher and new deckhouse fill the gap between the after funnel and gun turret.

(b) French *Surcouf* class destroyer. 1955–58. 2,750 tons. 422 ft. o.a. 34 knots. In this class there is some variation as ships are designed as radar pickets, anti-submarine vessels or anti-aircraft ships. Generally armament consists of 6 5-in. guns, 6 57-mm. and 6 20-mm. A.A. armament, 12 21·7-in. torpedo tubes and guided missiles.

(c) U.S. *Forrest Sherman* class. 1955–59. 2,850 tons. 418¼ ft. o.a. This is a new class of conventional destroyer in a navy which has well over three hundred ships of this type. It has three single 5-in. guns, two of them aft in an arrangement which is unusual in the U.S. Navy. There are 4 3-in. guns in twin gunhouses, 4 21-in. torpedo racks, and 2 Hedgehogs, for anti-submarine work. Speed about 32 knots. An unusual feature is that the whole of the ship's superstructure above the main deck is made of aluminium.

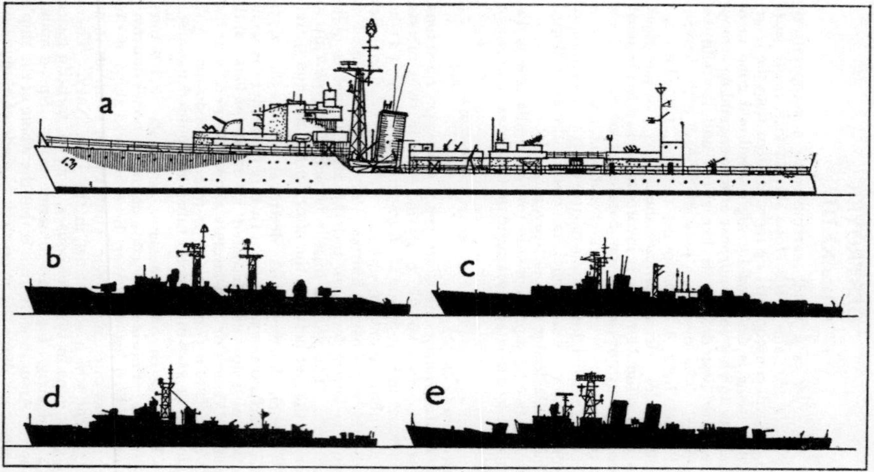

FIG. 51. Frigates

FRIGATE
(Plates XV and XXIII)

THE term "frigate" is now used for a wide variety of ships with a tonnage ranging from 1,000 to 2,000 tons and a range of speed from about 15 knots up to that of a destroyer. The frigate has no standard armament but is primarily used for anti-submarine duty and the escort of merchant vessels. The term is even more confusing with the United States present use of "frigate" for a vessel which at one time would have been classed as a light cruiser. British frigates included ships built as such, converted fleet destroyers, converted escort destroyers and many other types of small vessel. Modern motor frigates are designed as anti-aircraft ships for the protection of convoys. The dividing line between the fast frigate and the destroyer is almost impossible to define.

Illustrations (Fig. 51)

(a) Fast anti-submarine frigate *T* class, a limited conversion from a fleet destroyer. The silhouette is typical of the destroyer built during the 1939–45 war. 2,000 tons., 362 ft. o.a. 36·75 knots. Armament 2 4-in. guns in twin mounts, 7 40-mm. anti-aircraft guns, 2 Squids and 4 21-in. torpedo tubes.

(b) *Leopard* class anti-aircraft frigates. A post-war type, with diesel propulsion, equipped for convoy protection or general destroyer duties. A distinctive feature is the sudden drop in deck level forward which gives the effect of a merchant ship forecastle (also seen in some other modern British frigates). 2,250 tons. 340 ft. o.a. 25 knots. Armament 4 4·5-in. guns in twin turrets, 2 40-mm. anti-aircraft Bofors and a triple-barrelled Squid.

(c) *R* class anti-submarine frigate. Converted destroyers with tonnage of 2,200, a length of 358¼ ft. o.a. and a speed of 31·75 knots. Armament 2 4-in. guns in a twin mount forward, 2 Bofors guns, 2 Limbo depth charge mortars aft. This type is distinguished by a long forecastle deck extending to well aft of the mainmast and a long high bridge superstructure.

(d) For comparison with the latest types of frigate this drawing shows the smaller and slower *Bay* class. A number of them have been sold to the Portuguese Navy and four are in commission as R.N. survey vessels.

(e) One of the latest types of British frigate is the new *Tribal* general purpose frigate which is easily distinguished by her two funnels—almost equal in size—placed very close together. Steam turbines are supplemented by gas turbines to give additional power for bursts of high speed and to enable the vessel to start from cold in an emergency without the necessity of lying in harbour with steam up. 2,300 tons. 360 ft. o.a. 28 knots. Armament 2 single-mounted 4·5-in. guns, 2 Bofors and 1 Limbo mortar. A helicopter is carried to take off from, and land on, the small platform just forward of the after gun.

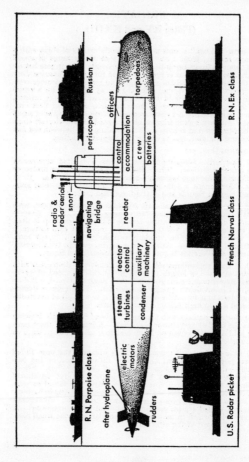

FIG. 52. Submarines

SUBMARINE
(Plate XIV)

THE essential feature of the submarine is its long cigar-shaped hull which has no large projection except the bridge and conning tower which forms a simple, compact shape. On each side of the hull are the blisters which contain the ballast tanks.

The torpedo tubes are fixed at the bows and stern, frequently 4 21-in. tubes each and in the more recent vessels they are of the homing type. (This new type of torpedo can be directed on to its target, by radio and other means, after it has been fired.) The conventional submarine is propelled by diesel engines for surface cruising and electric motors underwater, but the British experimental class ships are propelled by a new type of turbine using hydrogen peroxide as the main component of the fuel. With this development underwater speeds of about 25 knots are obtained. By 1967 the United States Navy hopes to have seventy-five nuclear powered submarines in commission following the pattern of their first which was launched in 1954. With the tremendous advantage of an almost limitless cruising range without refuelling, the atomic submarine can remain at sea for months and operate in any part of the world, even under the Polar ice. Another important development is the "Polaris" guided missile which can be launched either from the surface or underwater.

The introduction of the "snort" breathing tube makes it possible for fresh air to be taken in while submarine is cruising submerged just below the surface. The big U.S. nuclear powered submarines can usually be distinguished by the diving planes which project from the conning tower (sail or fin as it is now called in connection with the big new ships). The world's largest submarine is the nuclear powered U.S.N. *Triton* which has a length of 447 ft. and a speed of 30 knots both surface and submerged, so that she could keep station with destroyers and aircraft carriers and take her part as an early warning picket for task forces.

The first British nuclear powered submarine, with a length of 265 ft., was launched in 1960 and named *Dreadnought*. Instead of the traditional cigar-shaped hull she is more like a whale (*see* the drawing in Fig. 52) with a silhouette forward blunter than the usual submarine. Some submarines have a dome or other projection in the bows at deck level; this structure contains the underwater detection equipment known as asdic.

The new British submarines of the *Oberon* class have an underwater speed of about 25 knots, and for the first time glass fibre laminate is used for the superstructure.

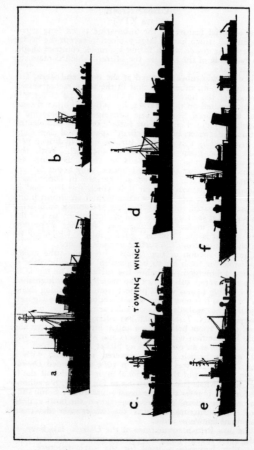

FIG. 53. Minesweepers

MINESWEEPER

DURING hostilities minesweeping may be done by different kinds of vessels, such as trawlers or pleasure steamers, converted for the purpose, but specially-built minesweepers are now classified into three groups: ocean, coastal, and inshore.

The illustration shows that the silhouettes vary considerably, but all minesweepers have two features in common, (a) the large towing winch placed abaft the superstructure and (b) the cranes or derricks at the stern. Sometimes the torpedo-like paravanes and rectangular otter boards may be seen also at the stern.

The smaller minesweepers are usually built of wood and fitted with non-magnetic equipment. Some United States coastal sweepers are equipped with diesels made of non-magnetic stainless-steel alloy.

In the 1939–45 war three types of sea mine were used. The *contact* mine was moored to the sea bed and floated just below the surface of the sea. It was detonated by direct contact but minesweepers cleared the contact mine by cables towed astern to cut the mine from its mooring. The *magnetic* mine lay on the sea bed and was activated by the steel hull of a vessel passing near it. The minesweeper could detonate it from a safe distance by electrical means. The *acoustic* mine was set off by the vibrations of the ship's propeller or engines and could be swept also by acoustic means.

Illustrations (Fig. 53)

(a) U.S. ocean minesweeper *Agile* class. 1952–56. 665 tons. 171 ft. o.a. 1 Bofors gun. 12 knots. Wooden hulls and non-magnetic equipment, non-magnetic stainless steel diesel motors. Many built for foreign navies.

(b) British inshore *Ham* and *Ley* class. 1952 onwards. c. 100 tons. 106½ ft. o.a. *Ham* class of wood. *Ley* composite.

(c) British coastal *Ton* class. 1953 onwards. 360 tons. 152 ft. o.a. 15 knots. Wooden hull.

(d) United States Fleet *Auk* class. 1942–44. 890 tons. 221¼ ft. o.a. 18 knots. 1 3-in. gun. In reserve.

(e) French coastal *Flower* class. 1953 onwards. Built U.S.A. 370 tons. 141 ft. o.a. 14 knots (8 knots sweeping). Wooden hulls.

(f) Russian *Vasili Gromov* class. 1940–50. 600 tons. 250 ft. o.a. 2 4-in. guns. A.A. 24 knots.

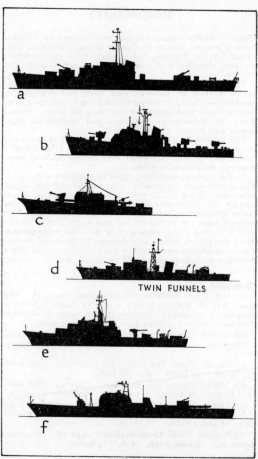

TWIN FUNNELS

Fig. 54. Light coastal craft

THESE small fast ships are assigned to many duties in inshore waters: anti-submarine patrol, reconnaissance, harbour defence, air-sea rescue and offensive patrol with guns or torpedoes. They are powered by diesels, petrol engines or gas turbines.

Illustrations (Fig. 54)

(a) French *Le Fougueux* class patrol vessel (1954–59) is comparatively large with a tonnage of 325 and an overall length of nearly 180 ft. Their outline may in difficult light appear like a frigate. Armament consists of 2 Bofors A.A. guns and anti-submarine mortars. Speed 18·5 knots.

(b) Italian motor gunboat. 1963. This is a 40-knot boat propelled by diesel and gas turbines and can be used in one of three rôles: *gunboat* with 3 Bofors guns and rocket launcher; *torpedo boat* with 4 21-in. torpedoes and 1 Bofors gun; *fast minelayer* with 1 Bofors and 8 mines.

(c) British *Brave* class fast patrol boat. 1960. Also a convertible vessel used either as a *motor torpedo boat* with 4 side-launched 21-in. torpedoes or as a *motor gunboat* with 2 Bofors guns and only 2 torpedoes. 89 tons' standard displacement, a length of 98 ft. o.a. and remarkable speed of 50 knots, powered by gas turbines.

(d) British seaward defence boat, *Ford* class. 1956 onwards. 120 tons. 117 ft. o.a. 15 knots. This new type of coastal warship is designed to defend estuaries and harbours from enemy submarines and it is therefore well equipped with electronic detection gear of the latest kind. It is armed with a single Bofors gun and a triple-barrelled Squid or depth charges.

(e) Danish seaward defence craft. 1960–61. 150 tons. 121 ft. Armed with a Bofors gun and depth charges and propelled by diesel engines giving a speed of about 20 knots.

(f) Swedish convertibles. 1951 onwards. 155 tons. 157 ft. These diesel boats have speeds up to 37 knots and like (b) and (c) can be used either as motor torpedo boats or gunboats. Other Swedish torpedo boats are capable of more than 40 knots.

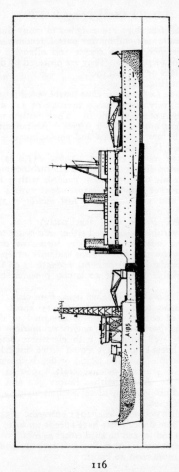

FIG. 55.   Depot ship, refitted as a nuclear powered submarine parent ship

DEPOT SHIP

In appearance the naval depot ship resembles a large merchantman with high topsides, many portholes and a number of heavy derricks or deck cranes, except that she is always painted grey like other warships. Her function is to serve as a "mother" ship to a group of particular warships such as submarines, destroyers or coastal craft. In recent years the U.S. *Proteus* was stationed on the Clyde as a depot ship (called a tender by the Americans) for a nuclear powered fleet ballistic missile submarine squadron.

The depot ship is equipped with extensive workshops, powerful cranes and all the materials required for servicing the relevant warships. In addition the submarine depot ships are fully equipped with accommodation, catering and recreational facilities for the submariners. A chapel, a hospital (with operating theatre) and a dental surgery add to the facilities.

Another form of depot ship is the accommodation ship, often an obsolete passenger liner, in a permanent position in a naval port. The French battleships *Jean Bart* and *Richelieu* are disarmed and used as port accommodation ships, or barracks, at Toulon and Brest respectively. Other French warships are used for similar purposes at Toulon.

The larger submarine or destroyer depot ships are quite heavily armed in spite of their non-offensive function. The British examples have 6 to 8 4·5-in. guns and Bofors anti-aircraft guns. The U.S. Navy tenders have 5-in. guns and similar A.A. armament.

Fig. 55 shows the reconstructed *Maidstone* (9,100 tons, 530 ft. o.a.) now to be used as the parent ship for the nuclear powered submarine *Dreadnought*. Her sister *Forth* is under refit for the same purpose.

Akin to the depot ship is the heavy repair and maintenance ship (*see* Fig. 56a), similar in function and appearance except that she does not have the accommodation and facilities mentioned above. This type is rarely built for the purpose but is usually a converted passenger liner, although the R.N. uses an ex-aircraft carrier for this purpose.

x = GOAL - POST MAST

FIG. 56. Repair ships and naval auxiliaries

THE vessels illustrated in Fig. 56 are all auxiliary to the needs of the fighting ships. The two repair and maintenance ships, (a) and (d), fly the White Ensign while the others fly the Blue Ensign defaced by a gold anchor (*see* page 24). All those illustrated are merchantmen in appearance with some distinctive differences due to their specific functions. Fleet auxiliaries are painted with black or grey hulls, grey superstructure and light grey funnel with a black top.

The HEAVY REPAIR SHIP (a) is an ex-Cunard passenger liner, but the heavy cranes fore and aft, and small gun platforms, alter her silhouette.

The FAST FLEET REPLENISHMENT OILER is a large oil tanker, but her three sets of goal-post masts are fitted for handling hose gear as her main function is to transfer oil and stores to a warship while both are under way. The oiler takes up a position on a steady course and speed at a convenient distance from the warship. In order to reduce motion they both steam into the wind or the direction of the sea, whichever is the stronger. After contact is made by firing a nylon line across the gap, the oil hoses are sent across. Solid stores can also be transferred while at speed. The new vessel shown (b) was built in 1963 with a length of 583 ft. and is propelled by steam turbines.

The FLEET ATTENDANT OILER is a smaller vessel, in this instance (c) with a length of 286 ft. o.a. and driven by triple expansion steam engines giving a speed of 12 knots. This type has a much heavier superstructure than the merchant tanker (page 65).

The drawing (d) shows a naval MAINTENANCE SHIP converted from a wartime standard merchant ship (Fig. 18a). Like the ex-liner mentioned above she has heavy cranes and a welter of other deck equipment.

The COASTAL SALVAGE VESSEL (e) is easily distinguished by her large horns at the bows and heavy derricks amidships. This example is capable of lifting up to 200 tons dead weight directly over the bows.

The Admiralty, and in fact most navies, possesses a fleet of powerful tugs similar in function and appearance to the commercial ocean and harbour tug (see page 75). In wartime they usually carry a 3-in. gun and A.A. light guns. It is an interesting fact that in recent years the Admiralty has introduced diesel-electric *paddle* tugs for harbour work in the dockyards. The drawing (f) shows a FLEET TUG built in 1956 capable of 13 knots, propelled by diesels and fitted with variable pitch propellers.

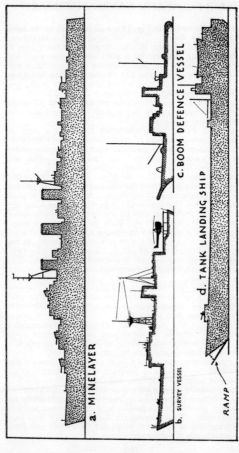

a. MINELAYER

b. SURVEY VESSEL

c. BOOM DEFENCE VESSEL

d. TANK LANDING SHIP

RAMP

FIG. 57. Miscellaneous naval vessels

(a) MINE COUNTERMEASURES SUPPORT SHIP (previously a Minelayer). 2,650 tons. 418 ft. 37–40 knots. Armament reduced to 4 40-mm. guns.

This vessel resembles a cruiser in outline and is the fastest type of large warship.

(b) SURVEY VESSEL. 850 tons. 230 ft. 17 knots. No armament.

The drawing shows the British survey vessel H.M.S. *Vidal* (1,885 tons, 315 ft.), the first to be designed for hydrographic surveying and chart production. She carries an eight-seater helicopter and is painted in the International Survey colours: pale grey hull with black riband, yellow funnel and white upperworks.

(c) BOOM DEFENCE SHIP. 730 tons. 175 ft. 11 knots. 1 3-in. gun.

The boom defence vessel may either patrol antisubmarine defences and attend to minor repairs to buoys and nets, or she may remain in position permanently at the gate through the defences.

(d) TANK LANDING SHIP. 1,600 tons. 328 ft. 11 knots. Light A.A.

An entirely new class of warship, mass-produced during the 1939–45 war. The important feature is the hinged ramp at the bows which when raised closes the mouth of the hold and when lowered allows motor vehicles, tanks, etc., to be run directly on to the beaches. Since the war converted vessels have been employed commercially carrying lorries between Preston and Larne, Tilbury and the Continent, Southampton and Cowes. In 1957 a similar vessel carried vehicles from New York to St. Nazaire on the same principle of drive on and drive off.

FIG. 58. T.S.S. *Nevasa*

The T.S.S. *Nevasa* is a modern British transport built in 1956 and operated by the British India Line. She has a tonnage of 20,527 g.t., a length of 609 ft., and her turbines give her a speed of 17 knots. The *Nevasa* is the largest and fastest ship to have been built solely for trooping. She is capable of carrying 1,500 troops, but her future is uncertain as other troopships have been disposed of.

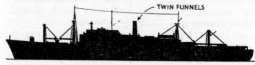

FIG. 59. U.S. *Barrett* class

The newest United States transports are 20-knot vessels with a displacement of 17,600 tons and a length of 533 ft. o.a. The distinguishing feature is the pair of slender tapered funnels placed abreast

FIG. 60. U.S. *General* class

The United States *General* class of troop transports is a group of vessels with a standard tonnage of about 11,000 tons and a length of 622 ft. o.a. These 17-knot ships are able to carry up to 3,000 troops. Although they have engines aft they have a broken silhouette which prevents confusion with the oil tanker. Other *General* transports resemble normal passenger liners.

THE troopship is a passenger liner converted, either temporarily or permanently, to carry a large number of soldiers or airmen. In peace-time the hull is painted white, the funnels buff, and she has a broad blue band round the upper part of the hull. Some well-known peacetime troopers were operated by the Bibby Line; *Lancashire*, with a gross tonnage of 9,500 tons, carried about 1,500 troops per voyage to the Far East. During the war many passenger liners were used for trooping, among them the *Queen Elizabeth* (Fig. 12a). She was completed after the war had started and was immediately put into service as a troopship when she successfully carried many thousands of troops across the North and South Atlantic. The *United States* (*see* Fig. 12c) was built as a dual-purpose ship to carry 14,000 troops in times of war.

In recent years some well-known troopships have been taken off trooping and fitted out as educational cruise ships. This, in the main, is due to increased use of air transport for conveying troops to the Far East and elsewhere.

The hospital ship is another converted passenger liner. She is painted white and has a broad green band and a number of large red crosses round the upper part of the hull. During the war many cross-Channel passenger ships were converted to hospital ships.

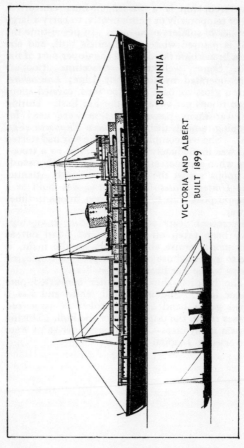

BRITANNIA

VICTORIA AND ALBERT
BUILT 1899

FIG. 61. Royal yacht *Britannia*

ROYAL YACHT *BRITANNIA*

THE royal yacht *Britannia* was built by John Brown Ltd. of Clydebank and was accepted by the Admiralty in January 1954, nine months after she had been launched by Her Majesty the Queen.

The *Britannia* was designed as a dual-purpose vessel: for the peace-time rôle of conveying members of the Royal Family to any part of the globe and for the war-time rôle of naval hospital ship when her stabilizers, special air-conditioning and large laundry would be of special importance. She has two sets of turbines modelled on those made for fast cross-Channel packets giving her a continuous sea speed of 21 knots. She has a gross tonnage of 5,769 and an overall length of 412 ft. 3 in. Special attention has been given to the design of the funnel to ensure the minimum interference from smoke and waste gases; the funnel and superstructure above the bridge deck are constructed of aluminium alloy.

The *Britannia's* royal apartments are placed aft between the main and mizzen masts. Custom demands three masts as when the Sovereign is on board the following flags must be worn: Royal Standard at the main, Lord High Admiral's flag at the fore and Union Flag at the mizzen. The White Ensign is always flown at the stern.

The small drawing shows the silhouette of the royal yacht *Victoria and Albert* which was built in 1899 and scrapped in 1954. She had a displacement of 4,700 tons and was capable of a speed of 20 knots. Her ornamental binnacle, from the earlier *Royal George*, is now on the *Britannia*.

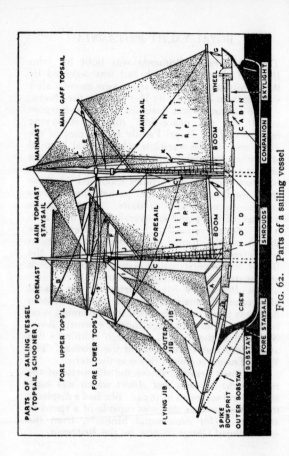

PARTS OF A SAILING VESSEL
(TOPSAIL SCHOONER)

MAIN GAFF TOPSAIL

MAIN TOPMAST
STAYSAIL

MAINMAST

MAINSAIL

WHEEL

SKYLIGHT

COMPANION

CABIN

BOOM

SHROUDS

HOLD

BOOM

FORESAIL

FOREMAST

FORE UPPER TOPS'L

FORE LOWER TOPS'L

FLYING JIB

OUTER JIB

JIB

CREW

FORE STAYSAIL

BOBSTAY

SPIKE BOWSPRIT

OUTER BOBSTAY

FIG. 62.   Parts of a sailing vessel

126

5 — SAIL

PARTS OF A SAILING SHIP
(TOPSAIL SCHOONER)
(Plate XXVI)

RIGGING

A. Jib and forestaysail sheets
B. Upper and lower topsail braces
C. Fore braces
D. Fore sheet
E. Main peak halliards
F. Fore peak halliards
G. Main sheet
H. Main boom topping lift
I. Forestay
J. Fore topmast backstay
K. Main topmast backstay
L. Signal halliards
R.P. Reef points

Rigging can be divided into two categories: standing rigging which helps to maintain masts in their permanent positions, and running rigging which controls the movement of yards and sails.

STANDING RIGGING

A forestay passes from the top of a mast downwards in a forward direction.

A backstay passes from the top of a mast downwards to both sides of the vessel to take the forward strain of the mast.

Shrouds pass from the top of a mast (or a point on it) to the ship's sides.

Ratlines are short lengths of line which cross the shrouds at intervals to form ladders to the upper parts of the masts.

A lift takes the weight of a yard or boom.

Halliards raise or lower a spar or sail, or may be used for signal flags.

Braces control the fore-and-aft movement of the yards.

Clew lines lift the lower corners of a square sail.

To *bend* a sail is to attach it to a yard or boom, and to *furl* it is to secure it temporarily to a spar by short lengths of line called gaskets. The spike bowsprit has generally taken the place of the more elaborate jib-boom bowsprit. The former consists of one spar only.

The names of the spars, sails and rigging of a large square-rigged vessel follow the same system of nomenclature as shown for the topsail schooner.

These are the names of the sails of a square-rigged mast, starting from deck level: *course, lower-topsail, upper-topsail, lower-topgallant, upper-topgallant, royal* and in some instances *skysail*. Names of masts of a four-mast barque: *fore, main, mizzen* and *jigger*.

In naming a sail the name of the mast comes first, followed by the name of the sail. For example: *fore upper-topsail* refers to the third sail from deck level on the foremast and *mizzen upper-topgallant* refers to the fifth sail on the third mast of a full-rigged ship or four-mast barque.

The *mizzen-course* is sometimes referred to as the *cro' jack*. Several giant five-mast barques have been built and their fifth masts have been variously called *after-jigger, after-spanner* or *pusher*.

FULL-RIGGED SHIP
(Plates XXVI and XXVII)

THE full-rigged ship is a sailing vessel with square yards and sails on all three, or four, masts. To be pedantic the term "ship" applies only to this kind of vessel.

This was the rig of most of the fine sailing vessels of the middle nineteenth century when the famous China clippers achieved a speed and performance never equalled before or since. The clipper was the result of improvements in hull form and rigging inspired by earlier sailing vessels of the New England coast. The hull had very fine lines, with a long run forward and aft to eliminate underwater resistance. These improvements meant a reduction in cargo-carrying space, but with a light and valuable cargo of tea this was not a disadvantage. As the ships carried large crews, the number of sails was increased, and to increase the speed still further, small studding sails were added to the fore and mainmasts.

One of the most famous of the tea clippers was the British ship *Cutty Sark*, built at Dumbarton in 1869, with a tonnage of 921 g.t. and a length of 212 ft. In those days of fast ships and record passages she made many journeys from China in under 100 days during the few years she sailed in the tea trade. On one voyage she made daily runs of 350 miles for several consecutive days, reaching a speed of over 16 knots—a speed far in excess of that of the contemporary steamer and in fact as good as the fast cargo liner of to-day.

Other well-known British and American clippers were the *Thermopylae*, *Taeping*, *Ariel*, *Sir Launcelot* and *Fiery Cross*. These are only a few of the fast full-rigged ships of the days when the sailing ship reached a state nearing perfection after a slow development over many centuries.

Soon after the opening of the Suez Canal the tea trade was taken over by steamers, and many of the tea clippers were transferred to the Australian wool trade, where they continued to make remarkable passages.

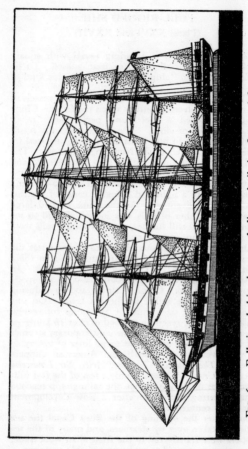

FIG. 63. Full-rigged ship; iron wool clipper built in 1877; 226 ft, 1,235 g.t.

As the wool trade developed the iron-built ships increased in size, and one of the largest clippers of her day was *Sabraon*, 2,131 g.t., length 317 ft., a giant compared with the small and delicate tea clippers.

The clipper *Cutty Sark* (Plate XXVII) made the best passages in the Australian wool trade, as she had in the tea trade; between 1874 and 1890 she averaged 73¼ days for seven passages.

The *Cutty Sark* ended her days in trade with a different name under the Portuguese flag. After lying for many years at Falmouth, and later in the Thames at Greenhithe, she has been entirely re-conditioned and dry-berthed at Greenwich near the Royal Naval College. The Glasgow-built full-rigged ship *Balclutha* (1886) has also been restored for the San Francisco Maritime Museum but she will remain afloat.

Several nations possess full-rigged ships as sea-going schoolships for either their naval or merchant services. Examples: *Sörlandet* and *Christian Radich* (Norway); *Georg Stage* and *Danmark* (Plate XXVI) (Denmark); *Dar Pomorza* (Poland). The sister ships *Amerigo Vespucci* (Italy) and *Cristoforo Colombo* (Russia) are ship-rigged but their hulls more nearly resemble the early nineteenth-century warship.

The last ship of this rig to sail under the British flag was the *Joseph Conrad*. She sailed round the world in 1934–36 as a privately run schoolship and is now preserved at Mystic, Connecticut. She had previously been the Danish training ship *Georg Stage*, replaced by a new ship of the same name.

FIG. 64.   Four-mast barque and a staysail schooner

FIG. 65.   Three-mast barque

BARQUE

By the end of the nineteenth century the barque rig had become popular. It differed from the ship rig in that the mizzen mast had fore-and-aft sails only and consequently a smaller crew was required. As at this time there was a shortage of crews, many full-rigged ships were altered to barques; it was found that they often gained in sailing qualities.

At the turn of the century the big barque had a measurement of about 2,000 g.t. and a length of between 250 and 300 ft. The hull form was less extreme than that of the clipper; maximum speeds were less, but the cargo-carrying capacity was much greater. At the beginning of the century seven huge five-mast barques were built; one of these —France II with a gross tonnage of 5,663—was the largest sailing ship ever to be built.

In the first two decades of the present century the sailing ship rapidly declined. Between the two wars a shipowner from the Baltic Åland Islands bought a number of barques and ran them in the Australian grain trade—undermanned and uninsured. Some of them carried cadets.

Some of the old interest in fast passages was revived when these ships were due in the Channel at the end of their homeward passage; the average time for the passage was not very different from that of some of the earlier crack ships. The following are some of the better-known vessels which belonged to this dying era of sail: *Lawhill* (1892); *L'Avenir* (1908); *Herzogin Cecilie* (1920) wrecked on the Devonshire coast in 1936; *Archibald Russell* (1905). The iron barque *Star of India* (1863) has now been restored as a maritime museum at San Diego, U.S.A.

The German four-mast barques *Passat* and *Pamir*, fitted with an auxiliary diesel and accommodation for 45 cadets, were employed for cargo-carrying as well as deep-sea training. Since the *Pamir* capsized in a hurricane in September 1957 with the tragic loss of eighty lives, the *Passat* has been withdrawn from service. In 1958 a new barque, *Gorch Fock*, with auxiliary diesels, was commissioned as a sail training vessel with the West German Navy. More recently the three-masted barque *Libertad* has been completed for the Argentine Navy.

Examples of three- and four-mast barques still used as sea-going schoolships: *Sagres*, ex-*Guanabara* of Brazil (Portugal); *Eagle*, ex-*Horst Wessel* (U.S.A.); *Sedov* (Russia); *Statsraad Lehmkuhl* (Norway); *Nippon Maru* (Japan); *Tovarisch* ex-*Gorch Fock* (Russia).

FIG. 66. Brig

BRIG

THE brig was a two-mast sailing vessel with square sails on each mast, and fore-and-aft staysails, jibs and spanker. This was a common rig for coastal and short-sea traders of the last century. The well-known colliers from the Tyne to London were of this type.

Some of the fastest brigs were the fish carriers bringing cod from Newfoundland to Bristol in the early part of the last century. The average size of the brig was about 200 or 250 tons and about 130 ft. in length. Members of the author's family commanded and owned brigs of 196, 162 and 94 tons which were registered at King's Lynn and sailed from there to the Baltic ports.

The snow was almost the same as the brig, except that the spanker was set on a small mast close to and parallel to the mainmast. Later the term "snow" referred more to a Scandinavian type of hull.

The brigantine has two masts, the foremast fully square-rigged and the mainmast fore-and-aft rigged. A modern example is the *Wilhelm Pieck*, a 200-ton vessel built as a schoolship for the East German Navy in 1951. The term *hermaphrodite brig* originally referred to this rig, but the term soon dropped out of use.

During the late eighteenth and early nineteenth centuries the Royal Navy used all three of the above rigs for their smaller vessels. Some of the early brigs were particularly beautiful little vessels. Long after steamships were firmly established in the fleet, small brigs continued in use as training ships.

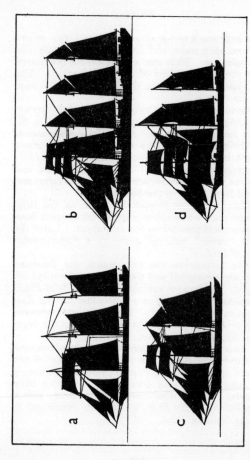

FIG. 67. Fore-and-aft rigged sailing vessels (I)

FORE-AND-AFT RIGGED SAILING
VESSELS (I)
(Plate XXVI)

THE three-mast topsail schooner (a) is a fore-and-aft rigged vessel with one or more square sails set on the foremast. This type is well illustrated by the Swedish schoolship *Flying Clipper* which was previously the British yacht *Sunbeam II*. She is quite often seen in British waters. The drawing (b) shows the Spanish schoolship *Juan Sebastian Elcano*, a large four-mast schooner built in 1927 with a displacement tonnage of 3,220 and a length of over 300 ft. The Chilean *Esmeralda* and the Brazilian oceanographic vessel *Almirante Saldanha* are similar.

After deliberations which have continued for many years, Great Britain is now to build a sail training schoolship. She will be a 300-ton steel, three-mast, staysail schooner (Fig. 64) with three square sails on the foremast. She will accommodate thirty-four boys and a permanent adult crew of nine. With a waterline length of 100 ft., the projecting stem and stern will give her an overall length of 135 ft. She will have a sail area of over 7,000 square feet and auxiliary oil engines.

The two-mast schooner (c) is distinguished from the brigantine by her gaff foresail and smaller number of square sails on the foremast. The French schoolships, *La Belle Poule* and *L'Étoile* (Plate XXVI), are good examples of this rig. These beautiful little vessels are modelled on the *terre-nuevas* which were employed in the Newfoundland cod fisheries. A very attractive two-mast topsail schooner may be seen along the south coast. She is the *Black Rose*, an ex-trading vessel built in Denmark in 1888 and now converted to a yacht.

The barquentine (d) has three masts, fully rigged with square sails on the foremast and staysails between the fore and main masts. Of the present-day schoolships, the Indonesian *Dewarutji* (1952) and the Belgian *Mercator* (1932) are barquentines.

The *Waterwitch*, 207 tons, 112 ft. long, was a well-known British barquentine built in Poole in 1871. She was the last part-square-rigged, cargo-carrying vessel to sail from a home port, continuing to do so until 1936. In the middle 1940's she was still trading in Baltic waters under the Estonian flag after a working life of over seventy years. In her later years in this country she was used as an unofficial training ship for pilots who were required by regulations to put in a certain amount of time in square-rigged ships.

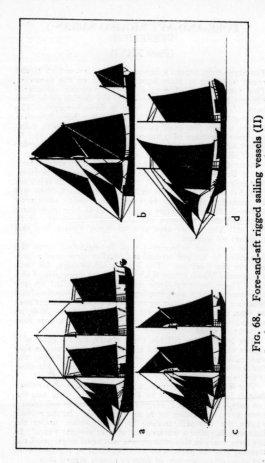

FIG. 68.   Fore-and-aft rigged sailing vessels (II)

FORE-AND-AFT RIGGED SAILING
VESSELS (II)

UNTIL the last year or two, a few auxiliary sailing schooners (a) and ketches could be seen trading in the Irish Sea and Bristol Channel. The last British wooden schooner, *Kathleen & May* (1900), carried clay to Eire or coal from the Mersey, and a few Irish schooners were also in the latter trade. One of the last vessels is the steel schooner *Result* (1893). Originally a three-mast schooner, her mainmast was later removed, but her elegant hull and "clipper" stem are unmistakable when she is seen, still trading, in the Bristol and English channels, often carrying granite chippings from Guernsey.

The Moray sea school *Prince Louis* is a three-mast schooner built in Denmark in 1944. She may be seen off the north-east coast of Scotland. Until recent years large numbers of Portuguese schooners were employed in the Newfoundland fisheries but their place is being taken by motor-propelled vessels.

The Thames spritsail barge (b) was once a familiar sight in the Thames estuary and along the Essex coast. Her huge mainmast and small mizzen were quite distinctive and so also was the large spar, the *sprit*, which supported the peak of the mainsail. Although these barges were up to 100 tons they could easily be handled by a crew of two. In 1957 there were twenty-three pure sailing barges (and many more with auxiliary power), but in recent years this number has diminished so that at present there is no sailing barge employed in trade. The annual Thames and Medway barge races, in which the trading firms competed, have taken place for the last time. Several of these interesting sailing vessels are now in private ownership and have been converted to yachts, so that this distinctive rig may still be seen.

The Portuguese trading ketch (c) is rapidly being replaced by powered vessels. This applies also to the typical Mediterranean ketch, the Greek caique (d), with her very pronounced sheer and high stem. Sometimes the caique has a balanced lugsail on the foremast instead of a gaff mainsail.

These fore-and-aft rigs are certainly disappearing from trading vessels all over the world, but many of them are preserved in yachts, either converted from them or built as pure pleasure craft. Some of the characteristics and variations of yacht rig are given in the following pages.

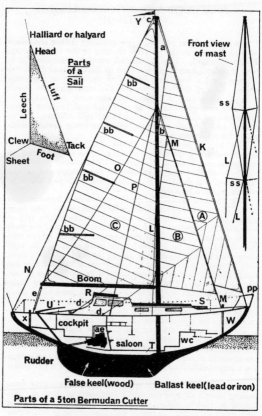

Parts of a 5 ton Bermudan Cutter

FIG. 69. Parts of a sailing yacht

PARTS OF A CRUISING YACHT

SAILS
A Jib (Headsail).   B Staysail (Headsail)   C Mainsail.

RIGGING (see also page 127)

K	Fore-topmast stay.	a jib halliard.
L	Shrouds.	b staysail halliard.
M	Forestay.	c main halliard.
N	Backstay.	d jib and staysail sheets.
O	Topping lift.	e mainsheet.
P	Runner.	

PARTS OF THE HULL

R	Sliding hatch on coach-roof leading down to saloon.	U Tiller, in some boats replaced by a steering wheel.
S	Forehatch to fore-castle.	W Anchor chain locker. X Locker.
T	Ballast under saloon floor.	Y Club burgee.
bb	Battens. pp Pulpit (protective stanchions).	
ss	Spreaders.	

The *saloon* or cabin is fitted with a settee along each side. The back of each can usually be swung up to form an upper berth.   In the centre is a cabin table.

The *forecastle* is a more confined space containing cot berths or on occasion the *galley* with its sink and gas stove.

The *toilet* may be either the chemical type, on a small boat, or a water-flushed closet in a compartment in the forecastle or aft.

The *auxiliary motor* (ae), using either petrol or oil, has a horsepower according to how the owner intends to use the boat: mainly for sailing or as a 50-50.   If the former the horse-power may be as low as 3 b.h.p.; 40 b.h.p. in a 40-ft. ocean cruiser and well over 100 in a power boat.

The *cockpit* is an undecked space aft with room for the helmsman giving easy access to the saloon.   The motor controls are in the cockpit.

The illustration (Fig. 69) shows a 5-ton cutter with Bermudan rig, an overall length of 27 ft. (21 ft. 6 in. on the water line) and a beam of 8 ft.   The three sails give a sail area of about 450 square feet.   The *galley* is on the port side off the *saloon*, which has a berth on each side, with cupboards and drawers underneath.

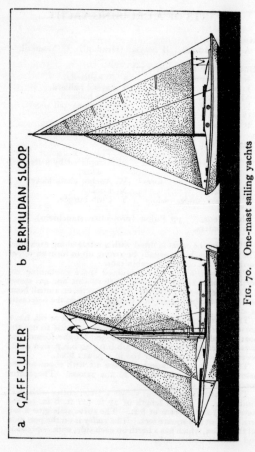

a **GAFF CUTTER**   b **BERMUDAN SLOOP**

FIG. 70.   One-mast sailing yachts

The pleasure yacht has a variety of rigs, many of them hybrids impossible to fit into any category. There are, however, four distinct arrangements: gaff cutter, gaff sloop, bermudan cutter, bermudan sloop. The gaff-rigged sloop with single headsail is usually a smaller boat. Two types are illustrated in Fig. 70.

(a) GAFF-RIGGED CUTTER (without topsail). The cutter is a one-mast boat with a mainsail, two headsails and a bowsprit. The gaff is a spar which supports the upper edge of the four-sided mainsail. It is derived from the spanker which was the result of the late seventeenth-century modification of the mizzen lateen (*see* page 179). It is typical of the older type of sailing boat and is still retained by many owners who prefer the gaff mainsail to the bermudan mainsail. The sail is reefed by lowering the gaff and taking in the slack by tying reefpoints near the bottom of the sail. The gaff has the disadvantage of extra top weight. It is always associated with a sturdy type of boat.

(b) BERMUDAN-RIGGED SLOOP. The sloop is a one-mast boat with a mainsail, one headsail and no bowsprit. The bermudan sail was introduced from across the Atlantic. It is a tall, narrow triangular sail and enables the boat to sail very close to the wind. The luff of the sail is not laced to the mast or hoops like the gaff mainsail, but is sewn on to slides which run in a metal track along the after side of the mast. This leaves no space between the edge of the sail and the mast. The sail is reefed by revolving the pivoted boom.

The bermudan sail is simpler to operate than the gaff sail, and has become the standard type for all modern racing yachts.

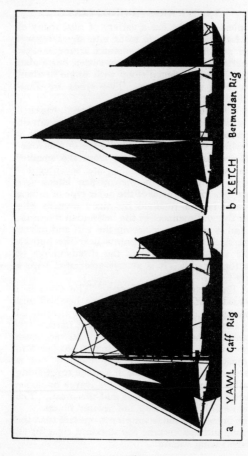

FIG. 71. Two-mast sailing yachts

THE schooner, ketch and yawl are all two-mast vessels with different arrangements of masts. The schooner has the forward mast either shorter than the after mast or the same size. The ketch and yawl have the forward mast higher than the other. The ketch and yawl differ in the placing of the smaller mizzen mast. The ketch has it well forward of the stern. The yawl has it abaft the rudder and sometimes almost on the sternpost or transom, when the sheet must be attached to a projecting bumpkin. Some yawls have quite diminutive mizzen sails.

GAFF-RIG YAWL. Fig. 71 shows a silhouette of a 30-ft. yawl with a canoe stern, high cabin roof, two gaff sails and two headsails. Such a boat could also set a main topsail. The yawl may be bermudan-rigged.

BERMUDAN-RIGGED KETCH. This ocean-going ketch has a counter stern, short coach roof, and triangular bermudan sails. The mizzenmast is stepped well forward of the rudder post. The gaff-rigged ketch was a very popular European fishing boat before the motor took the place of sail. Wooden ketches are fairly numerous in the Baltic, usually engaged in the transport of timber.

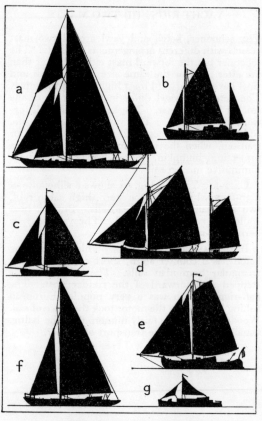

FIG. 72 Various yachts

146

VARIOUS YACHTS

THE main types of yacht rig have already been described, so that their recognition should not be very difficult. Over and above the standard rigs various craft have other characteristics which should make their recognition interesting.

Racing and cruising yachts are divided into certain categories relative to their length and sailing abilities (*see* page 149). The first drawing (a) shows a large 58-ft. yawl which according to the regulations of the Royal Ocean Racing Club is grouped under Class I for yachts between 36 and 70 ft. in length. Class II (f) includes those with lengths between 27 and 36 ft. and Class III between 19 and 36 ft.

Drawing (b) is a motor sailer of 45 ft. in length built for either sailing or motoring on a 50-50 basis. It is usually distinguished by a rather large deckhouse, less overhang at bow and stern than the pure sailer, and a comparatively small sail area.

Many pleasure yachts have been converted from working boats such as fishing boats—cutters, trawlers, quay punts—and pilot boats. Illustration (c) shows a Lancashire ex-fishing boat with a yacht-like hull which has made a most successful conversion. The converted Brixham trawler (d) is typical of the common fishing smacks which could be seen on the south and south-east coasts of England up to the early part of this century. Between 60 and 70 ft. in length, they are distinguished by a straight stem, deep counter stern and ketch rig. The converted Dutch boier yacht (e) has unusual features such as a curved gaff, leeboards and curved ensign staff (*see* Fig. 84b). Many of these craft are to be seen in British ports as well as in Holland and Belgium.

In addition to the standard rigs, and many conversions such as those described above, all kinds of hybrids may be seen. It is a common sight to see a ship's lifeboat converted into a cabin cruiser with a top-heavy cabin and a small steadying sail which is often quite ineffective (g).

FIG. 73.   Yachts: schooner *America*, 1851, and the royal yacht *Britannia*, 1893

The 12-metre yacht *Sceptre*, launched in April 1958, was the seventeenth challenger for the *America's* Cup, taken from Great Britain in 1851.

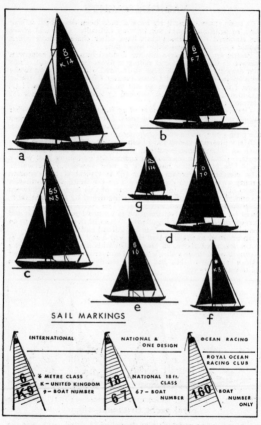

SAIL MARKINGS

INTERNATIONAL	NATIONAL & ONE DESIGN	OCEAN RACING
		ROYAL OCEAN RACING CLUB
8 METRE CLASS	NATIONAL 18 ft. CLASS	BOAT NUMBER ONLY
K — UNITED KINGDOM	67 — BOAT NUMBER	
9 — BOAT NUMBER		

FIG. 74.   Racing yachts.

RACING YACHTS

As a national and international sport, yacht racing is highly organized so that each entrant is classified either according to regulations which determine handicapping or according to a specific "one-design" class. The larger classes regulate length (*see* page 147), but within the class there may be some variation of hull form and rig. The smaller boats, however, are built to standard design so that all those in each class are identical. Many yacht clubs have their own one-design classes and some boats are confined to certain areas of the coast such as *Loch Long* in the Clyde, *Royal Corinthian* around Burnham-on-Crouch and *Q* class in the Solent. Others such as the *Flying Fifteens* may be seen in various areas.

The drawings in Fig. 74 show a few of these classes, and as they are all drawn to the same scale, their comparative sizes are clear.

(a) Usually pre-war and now used for off-shore racing or cruising, the 8-metre yachts may occasionally be seen. They have a length of about 50 ft. overall.

(b) The 6-metre, with a length of about 40 ft. overall, is raced internationally.

(c) The international 5·5-metre is a newer class which has become very popular. It has an overall length of 35 ft. and a sail area of 300 square feet.

(d) The *Dragon* is an international one-design class with an overall length of a little under 30 ft.

(e) The smaller *Swallow* one-design class, with a length of 25 ft., is distinguished from the *Dragon* class by a smaller jib and no cabin top.

(f) The *Star* is an international class which is raced in the Olympic games but is not so popular here as in some other countries.

(g) The *Flying Fifteen*—15 ft. on the water line—is a popular boat seen in many areas of Great Britain.

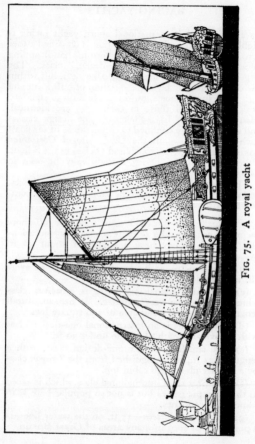

FIG. 75. A royal yacht

The classes of racing dinghy are too numerous to include here. Generally between 12 and 18 ft. in length on the water line, they are sloop rigged. Some of the following classes are well known: *International 14 ft., Firefly, British Moth, Snipe, Redwing*. The catamaran, a twin-hull, single-mast racing yacht, has become very popular in recent years, and even a trimaran, i.e. a yacht with three hulls, may be seen.

The diagrams at the foot of Fig. 74 show the general system in use for marking sails for identification. No further description is necessary, except to state that the national letter is usually the first letter of the country, e.g. D for Denmark, except for the United Kingdom which is K. In some national classes, the one-design category is identified by a symbol rather than a letter, e.g. *Snipe* by the silhouette of the bird and *Flying Fifteen* by f.f. in a V-shape.

This world-wide pastime stemmed from the royal yacht illustrated in Fig. 75 and described below.

ROYAL YACHT

AT the end of the seventeenth century the Dutch East India Company presented two yachts to Charles II of England. These yachts were similar to the craft which the Dutch had used for many years as fleet tenders. They had bluff bows, profusely carved and gilded sterns and a simple fore-and-aft rig (*see* page 179).

The presentation yachts proved very popular, and the king gave orders for fourteen others to be built in this country. They were like the Dutch models, except that the lee-boards were omitted, a square topsail was added and the hulls were given rather finer lines. The gaff mainsail became the standard rig for the English boats.

The king and his brother became enthusiastic about racing these yachts, and with their encouragement the foundations of English yacht-racing were laid.

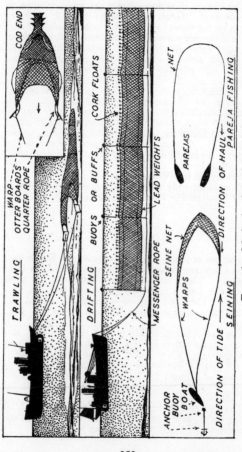

FIG. 76. Methods of net fishing

6 — FISHING CRAFT

METHODS OF FISHING

TRAWLING. The trawl is a large conical net that is dragged along the sea bottom. The mouth of the net may be up to 100 ft. across and is held open by the kite-like action of the otterboards, while the codend collects the catch. After several hours' towing the net is hauled in, the codend hoisted up by the gallows and the catch, of bottom-feeding white fish such as cod, plaice and haddock, is spilled on to the deck for sorting and packing in ice.

DRIFTING. The drift net is a long wall of net several miles in length that hangs in a vertical position. The pelagic, or near-surface, feeding fish such as herring and mackerel swim into it and their gills are caught in the mesh. When the nets have been shot at dusk the drifter rides to the nets, head to wind with a small steadying sail, and remains drifting until the nets are hauled in at dawn.

SEINING. The seine net has a centre codend and very wide wings. It is paid out and then slowly hauled in by an almost stationary boat and the bottom-feeding fish are driven inwards towards the net's centre.

PAREJA or PAIR FISHING. Two boats tow a deeply set net between them. It is then hauled in over the bows of both vessels, one of them finally hoisting inboard the nets and the catch—chiefly of hake. This method is commonly used off the north-west and south-west coasts of Spain.

LINE FISHING. Line fishing from small boats is a common practice in most parts of the world for inshore work and is used on a large scale in fishing from small boats, known as dories, off the Newfoundland coast.

In recent years new methods of fishing have been devised. A German system, still in the experimental stage, uses electronic devices and underwater lights to attract the fish, which are then drawn up into the fishing vessel by means of a suction pipe.

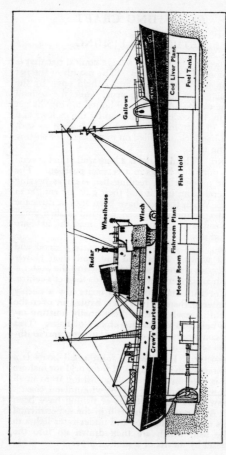

Labels on figure: Gallows, Radar, Wheelhouse, Winch, Cod Liver Plant, Fuel Tanks, Fish Hold, Fishroom Plant, Motor Room, Crew's Quarters

FIG. 77. Distant-water trawler built in 1958 with a length of 189 ft. and a speed of 15 knots. Sailing from her home port of Hull, she can remain at sea for five weeks. She is equipped with steam plant for melting ice, boiling cod livers to extract oil, and heating purposes

THE TRAWLER
(Plate XXX, upper)

THREE main categories of trawler operate from European ports:

(a) *Large* trawlers, with lengths of 140–190 ft. and 450–900 g.t., fish in *distant* waters such as Greenland, Newfoundland and Spitzbergen. With speeds of 16 knots the British ships can each bring back up to 250 tons of fish to their home ports of Hull, Grimsby and, to a lesser extent, Fleetwood after a round voyage of 3,000 miles or more.

(b) *Medium* trawlers, with lengths of 110–140 ft. and 190–450 g.t., operate off Iceland, the North Cape and the White Sea—areas known as the *middle* waters. Some of the fleets are based on Hull and Grimsby but the chief middle water fishing ports are Aberdeen, Granton and Fleetwood.

(c) *Small* trawlers, with lengths below 110 ft., fish in *near* waters such as the North Sea and the Irish Sea from Brixham, Lowestoft, Yarmouth and other smaller ports.

The trawler is engaged in all-the-year-round fishing and must therefore be a strong, sturdy vessel able to work in the worst of weather. She has a pronounced sheer, a superstructure that is placed well aft and a clear foredeck fitted with compartments, or ponds, for the sorting of the catch. When the net is hauled in the codend is suspended from the gallows and for this reason the bulwarks are unobstructed for most of their length. Another characteristic of the trawler is the powerful winch placed just forward of the wheelhouse: it may hold up to 900 yards of 3⅛-in. steel rope for towing the trawl net.

The modern trawler is a fine-looking, efficient vessel fitted with the latest electronic gear for fish-finding and for navigation. Propulsion is by diesel motors, diesel-electric units or by steam engines with oil-fired boilers.

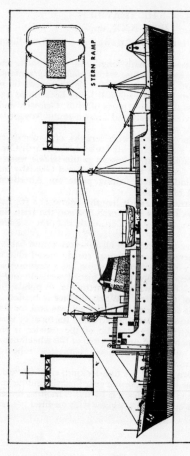

STERN RAMP

FIG. 78. *Fairtry II* is a stern-operating fish factory trawler built in 1959. With a tonnage of 2,857 gross, and an overall length of 275 ft, her diesel-electric machinery gives her a maximum speed of 12¼ knots

FISH FACTORY TRAWLER

ONE of the most important innovations in the fishing industry has been the recent British invention of the stern trawler, combined with the introduction of the fish processing ship. Instead of the traditional method of hauling in the net over the side from the gallows, the trawl net is hauled up a stern ramp which is similar to that of the whale oil factory ship (*see* Fig. 28). After successful experiments with a converted mine-layer just after the war, a Scottish company now has a growing fleet of specially designed fish factory stern trawlers similar to the one shown in the illustration opposite.

The new type of vessel is fully equipped as a factory so that the fish can be processed as soon as they are caught. About 40 per cent. of the catch is immediately washed, filleted, packed and put into deep freeze ready for the market and approximately 5 per cent. is converted into liver oil, while the remainder—offal and small fish—is made into fish meal for the farming industry. The British ships operate off Greenland and Newfoundland and can remain at sea for three months at a time. Other countries have adopted this type of vessel and Russia has a large fleet of ships similar to our own, which is part of the intensive mechanization of her fishing industry now being developed.

In addition to this type of large trawler small vessels are now built with a stern gallows and ramp to replace the usual side gallows (Plate XXX). The first British vessel of this kind was the Aberdeen trawler *Universal Star*.

FIG. 79.   Russian stern-operating fish factory
Puschkin

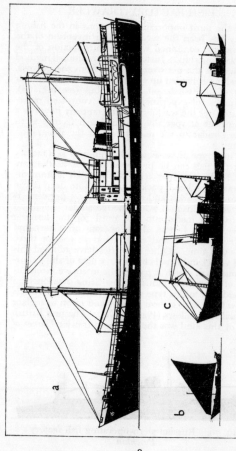

FIG. 80. Spanish and Portuguese fishing vessels. a. Grand Banks trawler; b. Portuguese long-liner; c. Spanish pareja; d. Portuguese sardine seiner

SPANISH AND PORTUGUESE FISHING VESSELS

THE normal distant water trawler, described on page 155, is exceeded in size by the vessel specially built for fishing the Newfoundland Grand Banks. The illustration (a) shows such a ship, built in 1955 as one of a Spanish fleet of Grand Banks fishermen, with a length of 235 ft., 1,360 g.t. and diesel engines giving her a speed of 10½ knots. With a hull strengthened for resisting ice, and excellent accommodation for a crew of 53, she is equipped to operate with a range of 30,000 miles. In general layout and appearance the Grand Banks trawler resembles the other large trawlers except that she has a long forecastle, a long bridge superstructure (of two decks) and a crow's nest on the foremast. Most of the vessels of this type are owned in France, Spain and Portugal.

The PAREJA (c) is a small fishing vessel with a clear platform aft on which the nets are handled, and a gaff and tackle on the foremast from which the nets are hung to dry. The modern pareja is usually a 100-ft. motorship with a comparatively high freeboard and is capable of about 10 knots.

The Portuguese SARDINE SEINER (d) is a small 53-ft. motor fishing vessel used in coastal waters, remaining at sea for no more than two days.

The Portuguese LONG-LINER (b) is a small open boat seen off the northern coasts of Spain and Portugal, sometimes under sail, but nowadays usually equipped with a motor engine.

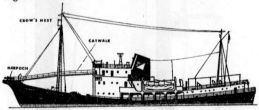

FIG. 81. The whale catcher (see also page 69)

THE whaler is distinguished from the trawler by a more pronounced sheer, larger superstructure, shorter foredeck, catwalk from forecastle to bridge and crow's nest on the foremast.

Fig. 81 shows a modern British-built whale catcher. Recent Dutch-built vessels have been powered by British free piston gas turbines.

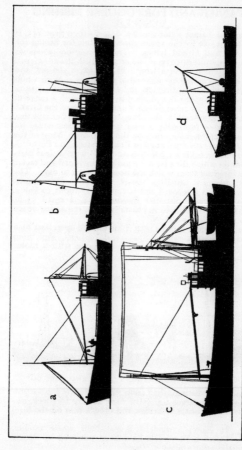

FIG. 82. Irish and Scottish near-water fishing vessels

SMALLER BRITISH FISHING VESSELS

THE large and medium-sized trawlers may be seen only at a limited number of British ports, but smaller drifters and seine-netters can be seen at many smaller ports round our coasts. Many of these are built as dual- or multi-purpose fishing vessels so that they need not be laid up through seasonal movements of the fish. The herring drifters follow the shoals which appear off Shetland in May and move down the east coast, arriving off the Norfolk and Suffolk coasts in October. There are also smaller herring grounds in the Minch, the Clyde estuary and the Irish Sea. The characteristics of the herring drifter are a powerful capstan forward, no forecastle, and a hinged foremast which can be lowered to improve the boat's stability. The small mizzen sail assists the vessel to keep her head to wind.

The Irish 50-ft. standard type boat (a) has a shallow draught and is designed for trawling, drifting, seining or long-lining. The larger Irish boat (b), 60 ft. in length (often built with the engine placed forward of the hold), is for seining or trawling.

Fleets of fishing vessels (c) can be seen in the Scottish north-east ports and in the western ports such as Oban, Mallaig and Stornoway. These are wooden motor-vessels built for ring netting (two boats working a form of drift net), drifting or seining. The seiners have a clear space aft of the wheelhouse for handling the nets, and there is a characteristic boom projecting from the side of the wheelhouse. The drifter can usually be distinguished by the large heap of football-like floats or pallets on the deck.

The boat (d) is a Scottish near-water 42-ft. trawler with a powerful winch aft of the wheelhouse.

FIG. 83. Built in 1957 with a tonnage of 131, *Ocean Trust* is a dual-purpose trawler-drifter registered at Yarmouth, and here shown as a drifter with steadying sail and lowered foremast.

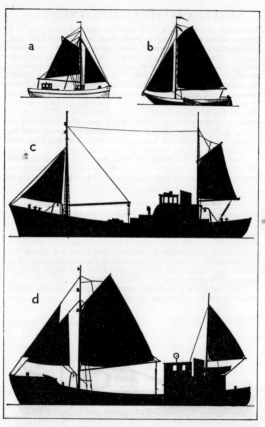

FIG. 84. Danish and Dutch fishing craft

DANISH AND DUTCH FISHING
VESSELS

FISHING in Denmark has always been of an individual nature and the Danes have developed their own distinctive type of craft. The single-mast wooden MOTOR CUTTERS (a) fish for plaice with the seine net in the North Sea. They have a high freeboard, marked sheer, a prominent wheelhouse and a canoe stern. The Danish 30–50-ton cutter is frequently equipped for trawling, purse-seining and long-lining.

The larger DANISH FISHING CUTTER (d), with almost twice the gross tonnage of the above, has a length of 100 ft. and carries a crew of six or seven men. Craft of this type are very seaworthy and often fish as far from their home ports as the Barents Sea and the west coast of Greenland.

In former times the Netherlands possessed a large number of small sailing boats which were engaged in inshore fishing for eels, mussels and other shell fish in the shallow waters of the Zuider Zee and the estuaries of the North Sea coast. They had interesting names such as HOOGAR (b), botter, schokker, tjalk and boier with characteristic features of sharply raked stems, short curved gaff, leeboards, curved rudder and flat bottom. The open motor-boat has taken their place, but these features can often be seen in this country in the boier yacht which is either built as such in Holland or an ex-fishing vessel converted as a yacht.

The modern DUTCH MOTOR FISHING CUTTER (c) has a steel hull 79 ft. long and is fitted with a Kort Nozzle rudder unit giving her a speed of 9½ knots.

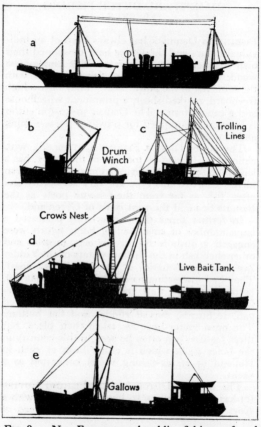

FIG. 85. Non-European rod and line fishing craft and a trawler

SOME NON-EUROPEAN FISHING VESSELS

THE unusual looking vessel (a) is a modern Japanese mackerel pole and line fisherman. A continuous platform projects from the two sides of the ship right up to the overhanging clipper stem. Live bait is used and during the night fishing sessions powerful lights are hung over the side to attract the fish.

The smaller British Columbian fishing vessel (b) employs two methods of fishing: trolling from poles and lines attached to the foot of the mast and netting by means of a seine net handled over the stern by a powerful drum winch.

The PACIFIC TROLLER (c) employs the trolling method with two or four rods and steel lines when fishing for salmon off the Pacific coast of North America. A similar method is used by the French tunnymen in the Bay of Biscay. Their rods, or tangons, are about 50 ft. in length and each one trails six to eight lines.

The TUNA CLIPPER (d) is a 130-ft. flush-decked launch with a low freeboard used for tuna fishing off the west coast of Mexico, central America and south California. Individual fishermen, each with his own rod, hook and line, fish from a platform which projects all round the hull. Live bait is carried in tanks on the deck close to the stern.

The NEW ENGLAND TRAWLER (e) has a length of 76 ft. and a speed of 9 knots. Working off the eastern seaboard of North America she makes about twenty trips each year fishing mainly for redfish.

All over the world there are numerous fishing fleets of varying types, but they tend to conform to the main categories already described. The method of fishing employed—whether trawling, drifting, ring netting, seining, long-lining, trolling or rod fishing—will determine their size and characteristics.

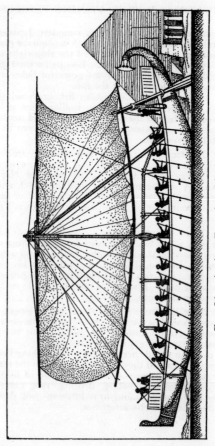

FIG. 86. Ancient Egyptian ship (1500 B.C.)

7—HISTORY

THIS section gives a brief general outline of the development of ship design through the centuries. Generally only the largest ships of each main historical period have been chosen for illustration, to show the distinctive features of each type.

ANCIENT EGYPT

MUCH of the information about the ships of the Ancient Egyptians is revealed by their wall paintings and low-relief carvings, and by their custom of placing models of houses, ships and human beings in many of the royal tombs.

In conventional drawings and carvings of the human figure, the Egyptian artist used a strange mixture of front and side views of the same subject, such as a head in profile with a front view of the eye. Drawings of ships were similarly distorted. The hull was always drawn in a side view with the sail in a fore-and-aft position, whereas when in use the sail was at right angles to the line of the ship, with the wind dead astern. Many of the drawings are of ceremonial ships, but there is plentiful evidence that the general cargo carriers and warships were very similar, remaining unchanged for many centuries.

Egyptian boatbuilders, handicapped by lack of timber, used short pieces of wood, even bundles of reeds, fastened together by wedges and dowels. A large rope truss was carried on posts from stem to stern to prevent the hull moving out of shape, particularly at the ends. This hogging truss was a typical feature and provided the main longitudinal strength of an otherwise weakly constructed hull. The foot of the sail was lashed to a two-piece spreader. When the sail was not used, oarsmen provided the motive power. The ship was steered with one or two long oars over the sides close to the stern.

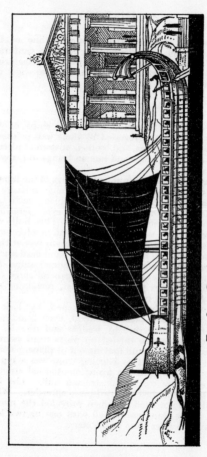

FIG. 87. Grecian galley (fourth century B.C.)

THE Greeks had two main types of ship—the galley and the sailing ship. The galley served as a warship and was essentially a large rowing boat with a sail for favourable winds. The sailing ship had no oars and was used principally as a merchant ship.

The Greek galley was long and narrow with a strong beak-shaped ram at the stem and a high, curved and often much-decorated stern post. The earliest boats had one bank of oars on each side, but later two, three or more banks were employed. The *bireme* had two banks with as many as thirty oarsmen to each—a total of about 120 for the whole vessel. The *trireme* had three banks of oars on each side, and was 150 ft. long with a beam of about one-tenth, or one-eighth, of that length.

There is still much conjecture about the exact dimensions of these vessels and about the arrangement of the oars. According to legend the mythical ships had ten or more banks of oars and were able to maintain a high speed over long periods.

As the artists and poets of the time were not so interested in the ordinary sailing ship, we have much less information about this essential craft. She was smaller than the galley, had one large square sail and two steering oars, and was slower than the oar-propelled warship.

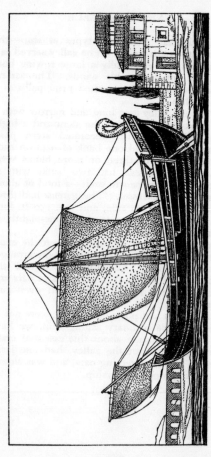

FIG. 88. Roman merchant ship (second century A.D.)

THE Romans used both galleys and sailing ships. The galleys in particular resembled those of the Greeks. The high decorated stern post was given more importance and the arrangements for the steersman were more elaborate.

The merchant sailing ships were small, rarely exceeding 100 ft. in length, with a broad beam to give good cargo-carrying capacity. At the water-line the hull form was the same at each end. The upper part of the hull was strengthened by external wales which ran from stem to stern, and the stern post was carried upwards and often given the form of a swan with the face looking aft. The ship had two steering oars, each controlled by a short tiller which rotated the oar in the direction required. The heeling of the ship made the deeper oar effective.

The Roman merchant ship voyaged not only throughout the Mediterranean but presumably beyond that sea, and therefore was strongly and sturdily built. On the after part of the deck was a cabin, and the high freeboard and substantial bulwarks gave good protection from high seas. The vessel was fitted with a large loose-footed square sail and had a satisfactory arrangement of rigging which remained almost unaltered for many centuries. An interesting innovation was the "artemon," a form of bowsprit, on which was set a yard and a square sail. Although this must have improved the sailing qualities of the ship very considerably, the "artemon" fell into disuse, and nearly a thousand years elapsed before it was rediscovered.

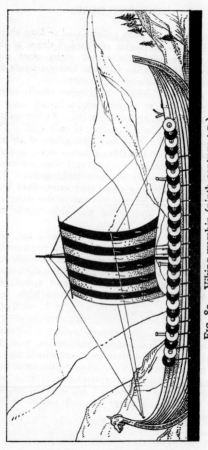

FIG. 89. Viking warship (ninth century A.D.)

NORSE LONGSHIPS

THE Viking ship was for many centuries the typical warship of northern Europe and was the type which invaded our shores during the centuries before the Norman Conquest. Its fine lines, beautiful sheer and turn for speed were to be lost to ship design until the sailing ship of the nineteenth century. Some of the distinctive features still survive amongst the small craft seen in north European waters.

To those interested in ships there can be no more thrilling sight than the Gokstad, Oseberg and Tune Viking ships still preserved in the Viking Ship Hall at Bygdøy, near Oslo. All three were dug from ancient burial grounds. The Gokstad vessel is the most interesting. When found in 1880 she was in a much better state of preservation than the others, and she represents a seaworthy vessel, while the Oseberg ship, although very similar, is believed to be solely a ceremonial burial ship. Five more Viking ships have recently been discovered in Roskildefjord, Denmark, and salvage work was started in 1962.

The Gokstad ship is 79 ft. long and 17 ft. wide, with a maximum depth of just under 7 ft. She had sixteen oars to each side, and a little lower than the gunwale on each side was a shield rack. At the time of burial sixty-four shields were in place, but only twenty-five were found when she was excavated.

The Viking ship was essentially a large open boat. The looms of the oars rested in ports cut away in the uppermost rows of planking, and these ports were shuttered when the sail was in use. When the wind was astern a heavy mast was erected and a large square sail hoisted. The vessel was steered by one oar over the starboard quarter. The ends of the hull were alike, and it was customary to continue the keel as stem and stern posts well above the gunwale level and to decorate them with carved, interlacing patterns terminating in an animal's head. The profile view scarcely shows the true beauty of the Viking ship, which was clinker-built, broad in the beam and very shallow, so that she sat on, rather than in, the water.

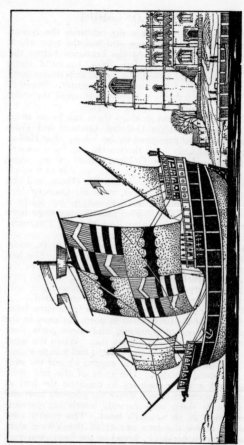

Fig. 90. Fifteenth-century warship

THE ships of the Norman period were very much like those of the Norsemen.

During the thirteenth century some changes, not all improvements, did take place. Most important was the introduction of fighting platforms or castles at the bows and stern, and a fighting top on the single mast. The charter seals of Dover (1284) and of Poole (1325) show typical fighting ships of the times, with some compression of the ships' form to fit the circular shape of the seal.

In time the ships became bigger, and the stern was raised still higher to accommodate more decks.

Ship design changed considerably in the fifteenth century—the illustration shows a warship of that time. Besides a very high stern she shows outstanding developments in the use of three masts and three sails and a rudder, hung on the stern post. The large square mainsail is like that of the Viking ships, and a Mediterranean lateen sail has been introduced on the mizzenmast. She has a bowsprit, like the Roman "artemon," but as yet no sail is set on it. The hull is bluff and has lost the fine lines of the earlier ships. The invention and use of cannon on ships determined many of the changes of this period.

During the Middle Ages, warships and merchant ships were much alike, as their functions were interchangeable according to the needs of the times.

In the early part of the sixteenth century, the three-masted ship, with two square sails to the fore-mast and the mainmast, one lateen sail on the mizzen and the sprit sail set under the bowsprit, was well established. This is the vessel shown on the present-day British halfpenny.

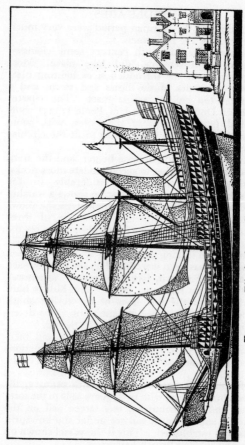

FIG. 91. Elizabethan galleon (sixteenth century)

SIXTEENTH CENTURY

MOST people know the names of some of the famous ships and seamen of the sixteenth century—the *Golden Hind* of Sir Francis Drake, *Ark Royal* (1588), *Harry Grâce à Dieu* (1514). During the prosperous reign of Elizabeth I, the British Navy became an important fleet, and played a large part in the rise to prosperity by such concerted actions as the defeat of the Spanish Armada, the individual and profitable exploits off the Spanish Main, and the voyages of exploration often combined with these skirmishes.

The ships were larger than in the Middle Ages but still, by modern standards, very small. The *Golden Hind* was about 75 ft. in length, and under 20 ft. in breadth, and although other ships were larger they rarely exceeded 800 tons. The Spanish galleons were similarly designed but were larger than the English ships and less handy in battle. Our information about these ships is gathered mostly from details of tonnage and measurements of men-of-war officially recorded at the end of the century. Shipwrights' draughts are extant of one ship only, and from these the model in the Science Museum was made.

The hull remained rather bluff but gradually became more streamlined. A prominent beak projected well out beyond the forecastle. The square transom stern was piled up with half-deck, quarter-deck and poop. The very marked sheer is a feature of the period, but gradually diminished during the next three hundred years. The armament was considerable—demi-cannon, cannon-perier, culverins, demi-culverins, sakers, and many intermediate sizes and hybrids of no standard pattern.

The ships were elaborately painted in bright colours with geometric patterns and motifs imitating architectural features.

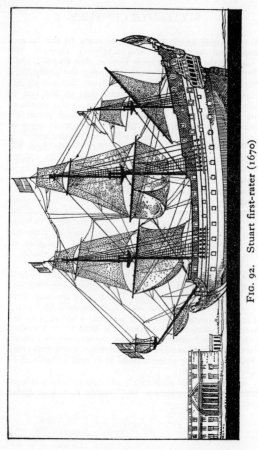

FIG. 92.   Stuart first-rater (1670)

DURING the seventeenth century warships and merchant ships were built much larger and, towards the end of the century, with many changes in design.

The more seaworthy Jacobean and Stuart ship resembled that of the previous century—the sheer and false beak were still prominent, but the stern was less piled up. The fourth bonaventure mast dropped out of use as more sails were added to the other three masts. The custom, which originated in the previous century, of dividing the masts into three sections still held and became standard in this century. This, besides meaning higher masts and more sails, was also an advantage in construction. In bad weather the topmasts and topgallant could be struck and brought down to the deck.

The usual sail arrangement on a typical ship was three square sails to both fore and mainmasts, a lateen with one square topsail on the mizzen, spritsail under the bowsprit and a small square sail set on a vertical mast at the end of the bowsprit.

In place of brilliant paintwork, fully carved and gilded decoration (known as gingerbread) was used profusely around the projecting stern and the quarter galleries.

The famous engraving by Payne of the *Sovereign of the Seas* (1637) shows these features very clearly. She was a large ship, almost twice as big as the galleon shown in Fig. 91. On each mast she set extra sails which were not adopted for all ships until a much later date. She had several lines of gun ports which do not follow the sheer of the ship—a deck on such a slope would be impracticable.

The large warships followed the pattern of the one illustrated (Fig. 92), but amongst the smaller warships and merchant vessels there was little change. They were usually of the three-mast and six-sail plan of the Elizabethan period.

The *Mayflower II*, built at Brixham in 1957 and sailed across the Atlantic to Plymouth, Massachusetts, the same year, is a full-size replica of a typical merchantman of the seventeenth century.

In 1961 the Swedish warship *Vasa* (160 ft.) was raised from the bottom of Stockholm harbour where she had lain since she capsized in 1628.

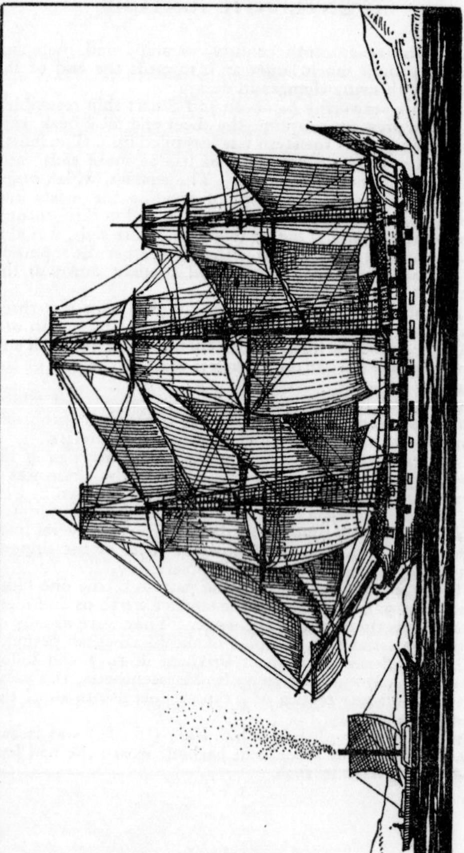

FIG. 93. Frigate of 1770

THE greatly reduced sheer was the most obvious difference between vessels of the eighteenth century and those of the previous century. The forecastle and poop were still higher than the waist, but even in the largest ships the poop was comparatively low. The gun decks more nearly approximated to the sheer lines, although at the stern they still differed. The *Victory*, with three gun decks, is preserved at Portsmouth. She was classed as a first-rater, i.e. a warship with 100 or more guns and 850 to 875 men.

The form and decoration of the stern and quarter galleries altered very little, except for a tendency towards simpler, more formal designs and less gilding. During the eighteenth century the carved figurehead became a feature of all sizes of warship. Particularly in sloops and frigates the lines of the hull became finer. On smaller ships the rounded bow took the place of the squarer beak-headed form of the large warships.

The sail plan was altered and improved. The triangular headsail was introduced, and it became customary to set a sail of this type on each stay. The frigate illustrated has three headsails and six staysails set between the masts. A small square spritsail was still set under the bowsprit, but the unwieldy sprit topsail disappeared. Side extensions were added to the top and topgallant sails, and were called studding sails. The mizzen sail, previously a triangular lateen sail, had the portion before the mast removed, resulting in the gaff sail as we know it to-day.

The merchant ships of the eighteenth and early nineteenth centuries, especially the East Indiamen and smaller West Indiamen, were similar to the warships and, being lightly armed, could be converted conveniently to warships when necessary. The hulls of the smaller ships, which still used the six-sail plan, were like those of the frigates and sloops with less decoration. Another type of this century was the bluff collier of about 300 tons. This was the ship sailed by Captain Cook in his voyaging round the world.

The smaller ship in Fig. 93 is the first European steam passenger ship, the *Comet*, built in 1812 on the Clyde. In 1962 a working replica of the *Comet* was built to celebrate her 150th anniversary and to form the nucleus of a maritime museum at Port Glasgow.

FIG. 94. Early steamship (1840)

NINETEENTH-CENTURY PASSENGER
SHIPS (I)

THE merchant sailing ship had been developing slowly throughout many centuries, and in the 1860s reached its highest degree of perfection. This stage was reached only after steam propulsion had been introduced, and already the days of the fast sailing ships were numbered. A typical clipper is shown in Fig. 63.

The first steam engines were fitted into hulls built for sailing ships, and for some time even new hulls retained the usual features of the sailing ship. Full sets of sails were maintained, partly to increase speed whenever possible and partly to cover the lack of confidence in mechanical propulsion.

The Atlantic was first crossed under steam alone in 1838 by the British wooden paddle steamers *Sirius* and *Great Western*. They arrived at New York on the same day, although the former had taken 18 and the latter only 14 days. On this voyage the *Sirius* carried 94 passengers, and when she arrived in America had used all her coal and was burning her spars. She made an average speed of just over 8 knots for the voyage.

Fig. 94 shows the first Cunarder *Britannia*, wooden-built on the Clyde. She crossed the Atlantic in 1840, and was the first steamship to carry mails from this country to North America, sailing from Liverpool to Boston in 14 days 8 hours, at an average speed of 8½ knots. She had two decks, and accommodation for 115 cabin passengers and 225 tons of cargo. She had a clipper hull, 207 ft. in length, and was rigged as a barque. The first Atlantic steamer built of iron and screw-propelled was Brunel's *Great Britain* which crossed the Atlantic in 1845, at an average speed of 9 knots.

The famous *Great Eastern* (1858) was a remarkable ship, five or six times as large as any other of her time. She was propelled by screw and paddles, and had six masts and sails and five funnels. Although she had a speed of 14 knots on the Atlantic service she was financially unsuccessful.

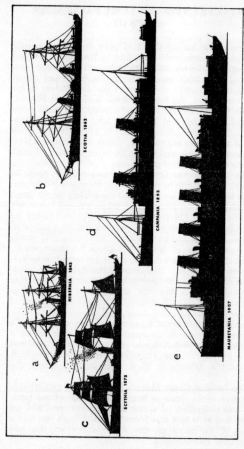

FIG. 95. Nineteenth-century passenger ships

NINETEENTH-CENTURY PASSENGER
SHIPS (II)

THE drawings in Fig. 95 give some indication of the changes in appearance, and increase in size, of transatlantic passenger ships throughout the second half of the nineteenth century up to the first few years of the present century.

(a) Wooden paddle steamer with auxiliary sail and clipper bows:

    Hibernia   1843   1,422 g.t.   248 ft.   11½ knots

(b) Iron paddle steamer with auxiliary sail and clipper bows:

    Scotia   1862   3,871 g.t.   400 ft.   14½ knots

(c) Iron single-screw steamer with auxiliary sail and straight stem:

    Scythia   1875   4,557 g.t.   433 ft.   13½ knots

(d) Steel twin-screw steamer without sail:

    Campania   1893   12,950 g.t.   622 ft.   21¾ knots

(e) Steel quadruple-screw steamer propelled by turbines:

    Mauretania   1907   31,937 g.t.   787 ft.   25 knots

As the success of screw propulsion became firmly established the large passenger steamers gradually lost the characteristics of the sailing ship, and were built to suit the needs of the new motive power. For some time masts and yards were retained; eventually only the masts remained. The stem was straight or slightly raked and the beak disappeared altogether. The stern was still like that of the sailing ship, and at first the officers' quarters and saloons remained aft, but later were transferred amidships. The navigating bridge was inconspicuous, and there was very little superstructure on those flush-decked steamers.

By 1890, twin-screw passenger liners were making the trip from Great Britain to New York in less than six days.

At the turn of the century the steam reciprocating engines of the Atlantic liners, still used in the modern freighter, gave way to the new Parsons reaction turbine.

Competition increased, and in order to attract custom more consideration was given to passenger accommodation. Rivalry was keen, especially on the Atlantic service, and owners and builders never relaxed their efforts to reduce the time and increase the luxury of the voyage.

The "Blue Riband" of the Atlantic service is an honour given to the ship which holds the record passage from Bishop Rock Light (Scillies) to Ambrose Light off New York. It has been held in turn by all nations interested in the service. The average speed has increased from the *Mauretania*'s 25 knots to 35 knots by the present record holder—the *United States*.

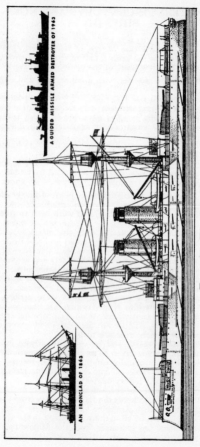

FIG. 96. Warship of 1902

AT the beginning of the nineteenth century naval shipping was dominated by huge slow men-of-war such as Nelson's *Victory*. The first-raters were three-decked ships with a high hull, very little sheer and over a hundred guns.

During the early part of the century many improvements were made in warship design, but the adoption of steam engines was long delayed. The smaller corvettes were the first naval vessels fitted with steam engines and screw propulsion. Except for the incongruous funnels they retained the external features of the purely sailing vessel. In the middle of the century France introduced the "ironclad," that is, iron armour plating on wooden hulls. This became a regular feature of most navies.

About thirty years later came the revolving twin gun turrets, housed in recesses below deck level.

Finally, with the abandonment of sails we have the battleship of 1900, as illustrated in Fig. 96. The hull had a ram and a single stern walk reminiscent of Elizabethan days. The armament was standardized—4 12-in. guns in twin turrets, a pair at each end of the central citadel, and many smaller guns, mainly of 6-in. calibre. The hull was fitted with booms and nets for protection against torpedo attack. The illustration shows the British-built flagship of the Japanese Navy, recently restored to her original appearance to be preserved as a national monument at Yokosuka.

The standard battleship quickly became obsolete when the revolutionary British and American dreadnoughts were constructed. The British *Dreadnought* had 10 12-in. guns, was propelled by steam turbines giving a speed of 21 knots, and was designed as a modern fighting ship.

INDEX OF SHIP TYPES

The Roman figures refer to plates

188

INDEX

INDEX OF SHIP NAMES AND CLASS DESIGNATIONS

The Roman figures refer to plates.

INDEX

191

INDEX

PRINTED FOR THE PUBLISHERS BY WILLIAM CLOWES AND SONS LTD
LONDON AND BECCLES

1604.664